medea's
daughters

medea's daughters

Forming and Performing the Woman Who Kills

JENNIFER JONES

THE OHIO STATE UNIVERSITY PRESS
Columbus

Copyright © 2003 by The Ohio State University.
All rights reserved.
Jones, Jennifer
Medea's daughters : forming and performing the woman who kills / Jennifer Jones. p. cm.
Includes bibliographical references and index.
ISBN 0-8142-0936-X (hardcover : alk. paper) — ISBN 0-8142-5114-5 (pbk. : alk. paper)
1. Murder in literature. 2. Murder in motion pictures.
3. Women murderers in literature. 4. Women murderers in motion pictures.
5. Women murderers—Case studies. I. Title.

PN56.M85 J66 2003
809'.93355—dc21

          2003006117

Other identifiers: ISBN 9780814251140 (paper)

Cover design by Former Factory Design
Type set in Adobe Electra

For Charlotte Weaver Jones
1915–2001

"Mere"

contents

acknowledgments — viii

introduction
Female Offenders and Offensive Females — ix

chapter 1
Petty (T)reasons for Killing Her Lord and Master — 1

chapter 2
Absence of (M)alice on the Victorian Stage — 19

chapter 3
A Jury of Her Peers — 39

chapter 4
Totaled Women: The Battered Wife Defense — 56

chapter 5
Medea Returns — 73

chapter 6
Narratives of Resistance — 88

afterword
Andrea Yates — 101

notes — 103
bibliography — 112
index — 121

acknowledgments

THIS BOOK IS built upon the excellent scholarship of many theater historians, feminist theorists, and legal scholars. I am particularly indebted to the works of Ann Jones, Mary S. Hartman, Faith McNulty, and Frances E. Dolan. Their meticulous research and keen insights have been invaluable to my project.

I would like to thank Dr. John Wolcott, Dr. Stephen Weeks, Dr. Barry Witham, and Dr. Sarah Bryant-Bertail of the University of Washington for their initial guidance on the project and for their commitment to the education of young scholars. I am also deeply indebted to Dr. Les Wade, Dr. Robin Roberts, and Dr. Sharon Weltman at Louisiana State University for their many thoughtful comments on the manuscript and for their excellent suggestions for revision. Their support and enthusiasm were invaluable to me. I am also indebted to Shannon Carey, Tara Mantel, Karie Kirkpatrick, and Heather Lee Miller for their help in polishing this manuscript and readying it for publication.

I would also like to thank two women whose friendship, intellectual stimulation, and unwavering belief in this project helped me to complete what at times seemed like a Sisyphean task. Tonia Steed and Dr. Jennifer Karas, you are indeed the godmothers of *Medea's Daughters*.

Finally, I could not have completed this book without the love and unending support of my husband and my family, who believed in me even when I did not. They are my greatest strength.

introduction

female offenders and offensive females

> The fear of the disobedient woman is the fear of the unwed mother; is the fear of the spurned wife turned to rebel; is the fear of the witch; is the fear of Medea.[1]

IN THE RICH DRAMATIC literature left to us by the ancient Greeks there are hundreds, if not thousands, of corpses. Many of the unfortunate met their death at the hands of a member of their own family; indeed, if one could pile up all the bodies of those murdered by their relatives in Greek tragedy, the mound would fill most contemporary stages. Adding more than her share of bodies is Medea, one of the most prolific murderers in Greek tragedy.

Euripides' Medea has walked our stages for over two thousand years, and she has, through repeated performance, become an icon for feminine criminality. Elaine Aston writes that "in terms of those 'classic' periods of theatre, where women have been absent from the stage, it has been possible to understand how the female has been constructed as a man-made sign in her absence."[2] And just as the "idealized woman" has been constructed onstage, so has her antithesis, the monstrous female, the Medea. When Medea first spoke upon the stage, a male actor in woman's mask and dress spoke the words of a male author. Like Clytemnestra before her, Medea's "man-made" monstrousness deflects the patriarchal acknowledgment of women's legitimate anger at being designated "less than" men. In this context Medea represents the perfect synthesis of criminal and feminist. She is the havoc women will wreak when they are no longer content to be submissive.

The woman who kills, in particular the woman who kills a member of her own family, has not only broken the law but has also violated gender expectations. Idealized "woman" has traditionally been constructed as self-sacrificing, passive, and nurturing; therefore, when actual women become violent, some sense must be made of their actions if the myth of feminine passivity is to be maintained. *Medea's Daughters: Forming and Performing the Woman Who Kills* argues that for over four hundred years, dramatic representations (plays and ballads, and more recently, television programs) have been used to contain and control cultural anxiety evoked by the disturbing figure of the female killer.

In her pioneering work *Women Who Kill* Ann Jones provides a recuperative history of the American murderess, and that book certainly sets the stage for my analysis. *Women Who Kill* provides a chronological exploration of famous (and not so famous) murder trials featuring female defendants and provides a feminist analysis of the ways in which those trials reflected and reinforced the subordination of women. *Medea's Daughters* builds on this important work by integrating a feminist analysis of the dramatic representations that circulated alongside, and often long after, the original trial.

Medea's Daughters draws on performance analysis and on theories of representation to enrich the judicial history provided in *Women Who Kill*. An intertextual analysis of the ways in which women who kill have been represented in the courts, in the press, and in the theater, *Medea's Daughters* explores the ways those representations have been used to reinforce women's subordinate status. This book emphasizes performance analysis, but analysis that includes the trial itself as a performance on par with the dramatic representations that followed it. This approach has the advantage of persistently invoking the material body embedded in legal and criminological discourse.

Theater historian Charlotte Canning has recently explored the ways in which the writing of history is as performative as the performances it attempts to historicize.[3] My analysis of the theatrical representations of real-life murderesses reveals how the performances themselves seeped beyond the purview of traditional theater history and became part of a larger cultural history of gender relations. As cultural theorist Annette Kuhn argues, "If representations always have use value, then more often than not they also have exchange value: they circulate as commodities in a social/economic system."[4] Each of the performances analyzed here has circulated along with multiple gendered messages from religious, legal, and scientific discourses that together have had a significant impact on women's lived experience.

Certainly there has been a lively debate in feminist cultural studies over the power of the image to reify ideology. Toril Moi questions the usefulness of "images of women" criticism to the feminist political project. "To study 'images of women' in fiction is equivalent to studying false images of women. The 'image' of women in literature is invariably defined in opposition to the 'real person' whom literature never quite manages to convey to the reader."[5] But as Stuart Hall shows in "Racist Images in the Media" and as Annette Kuhn articulates in "Power of the Image," there is a value in understanding how these stereotypical images impact power relations in a culture. "How we 'see' ourselves and our social relations *matters*, because it enters into and informs our actions and practices."[6] The act of looking at these murder cases in a feminist historiography performs a subversive gesture and provides a resistant reading to the encoded messages of the courtroom and stage. The analysis here is offered as an act of political intervention aimed at exposing the construction of gender ideology, which marks independent women as criminals and criminal women as monstrous. This history of murdering women, as Canning would say, "Resists and reveals norms by pointing to the production of those norms."[7]

Medea provides the starting point for this book and serves as my Ur-murderess. The ancient stories of her crimes laid the foundations for our current response to women who kill, and her name still evokes images of unchecked female rage. The accepted explanation of Medea's crime, a spurned and jealous woman taking revenge on an unfaithful husband, has endured for centuries, and it bears some examination.

Medea Past

> Medea revenges herself on Jason in the only way open to her; he has little regard for her love for him, but the children are his property, an extension of himself, of his identity . . . Medea has contrived a punishment for him *that no Greek woman would have dared*: in leaving him childless, Medea transforms Jason into an exile like herself, prophesying that he will die "without distinction."[8] (Emphasis mine)

In *Masters of the Drama* John Gassner describes Euripides' *Medea* as "A remarkable study of the conflict of the sexes, a penetrative analysis of the relative interests of man and woman, a powerful tragedy of frenzied jealousy, *Medea* is a landmark of realistic drama."[9] A feminist may be tempted to ask, what is so real about this man-made woman? As Gassner says, Jason's desertion leads Medea to a "frenzied jealousy" and to a desire to wound Jason as he has wounded her. As W. B. Worthen describes the murders he frames them as an "eye for an eye," a desire to even the score. Just as Jason's withdrawal left Medea an exile without distinction, so the murder of his sons will reduce him to a life "without distinction." This interpretation encases Medea in the role of wife and assumes that her life is destroyed when she is no longer Jason's possession. In this reading Medea's only option is to bring him down with her.

Medea does what "no Greek woman would do"; she is, literally, the foreigner, the barbarian, the Other. Her situation is juxtaposed with that of the women's chorus. These women sympathize with her abandonment but they tell her that, as difficult as it is, it is a cross she must bear with dignity. At the base of this choral (read communal) response is the assumption that it is *natural* for wives to suffer, and it is *natural* for men to discard the old for the new. What is *unnatural* is for a woman to strike back.

Medea's desire to punish those who would deprive her of her role as wife is seen as vindictive and unwomanly. Only an unnatural woman would rise against a system that is so much stronger than she. Her role as outsider and sorceress is central to the framing of her rebellion. Medea needs the aid of magic and sorcery to poison the "pure" womanhood of Creon's daughter. Medea's assertion of self is "foreign," "alchemical," and outside the boundaries of accepted female behavior. Medea's abnormality tacitly asserts the normality of women who *will* sacrifice their self for the good of their father/husband/son. A central theme in *Medea's Daughters* is that the criminal woman is defeminized in legal, journalistic, and dramatic discourse; they are separated from "normal" women, thereby reassuring the patriarchy that women embrace their submissive status. In *Acting Women* Lesley Ferris writes, "The plight of the wayward Medea, then, parallels the plight of self-willed Clytemnestra: both are denied the natural rights of motherhood by patriarchal justice, Clytemnestra's denial occurs in a civilized, apparently democratic trial. Medea, through her own violent actions, destroys her right, and eternally remains to prove the patriarchy right."[10] The only "right" Medea has is to motherhood, not selfhood. With descriptors like "wayward" and "self-willed," Ferris frames Medea's crime as impotent female rage—a violent rebellion that, when isolated in her "foreign" body, justifies the dominant culture's insistence that *their* women, the natural and true women, be submissive. Medea, like Clytemnestra before her, is the denaturalized woman who diverts the patriarchal acknowledgment of women's legitimate anger at being designated as "less than" men, by framing all feminine anger as both foreign and deadly. She is the dramatic mother of the women in this book.

Narratives of Containment

Cultural historians have long noted that the retelling or reenacting of crime stories reinforces existing power relations and maintains the status quo. When an audience hears or sees a criminal—who by definition has transgressed social norms—put on trial and convicted, those social norms are reinscribed. Legal historian Janice Schuetz writes that "popular trials reflect the values of the context in which they take place. In a sense they are complex texts illuminating the ways people reason in a defined time, place and community."[11] When the defendant is a woman, these trials also expose cultural anxieties over the place of women in society.

In *The Mythology of Crime and Criminal Justice* Victor Kappeler notes that when traditional beliefs are under attack, representations of crime in popular culture proliferate. "The subjects of [crime] myths are characterized as constituting a major threat to middle-class values, norms, or lifestyles. Myths of crime and justice when blended with threats to religious beliefs, economic systems, sexual attitudes or orientation, the traditional family, or political preference become a volatile mix."[12] Kappeler goes on to say, "The argument is simple; a growing menace is plaguing society. Not only is the conduct the preference of a deviant group, it is affecting innocents and endangering tradition."[13] In times of feminist resistance the murderess appears in plays and films, on the front pages of newspapers, and on the evening broadcasts in numbers totally disproportionate to her actual existence. The cases of the women studied in this book focus on disruptive and dangerous women who threaten the institutions of marriage, motherhood, and filial duty. Their cases received far more press than comparable murder trials in which men killed their wives, mistresses, or daughters.

Many have read the massive public attention paid to the trials and sentencing of these women as indicating a concern for a rise in female crime in the given cultural moment, but I believe that the popularity of dramatic representations of criminal women has little relation to any actual increase in female criminality. This book argues that dramatic representations of criminal women proliferate in times of feminist activity because they contain anxiety about gender roles and, in so doing, deflect attention away from the systematic repression of women.

Our intense preoccupation with certain kinds of crime and our studied ignorance of others clarifies our moral boundaries and, more importantly, articulates the power structures inherent in the drawing of those boundaries. For example, images of the powerless violently usurping privilege proliferate in our popular culture: in best-selling novels young black men who live in dangerous neighborhoods rob and assault affluent whites (*Bonfire of the Vanities*); on movie screens lesbians seduce men and murder them with ice picks (*Basic Instinct*); on the television battered wives kill their sleeping husbands (*The Burning Bed*). Kappeler argues that images like these serve to generate "moral panics,"[14] and they remind a nervous populace daily that a criminal element is threatening all that is good and natural in our society (e.g., white privilege, heterosexuality, and the sanctity of marriage). That 90 percent of homicides are intraracial, with black and Latin American populations constituting a disproportionate share of both victims and offenders, or that gays and lesbians are routinely the victims rather than the perpetrators of violent attacks, or that women are three times more likely to be killed by their husbands than to kill them, is not reflected in the popular representations of crime.[15] In the midst of the moral panics generated by a proliferation of crime narratives, the rich robbing the poor and the strong suppressing the weak goes unnoticed and uncriminalized.

Medea's Daughters focuses on the legal, cultural, and dramatic representations of six women accused of murdering an intimate. Each of their trials became national obsessions and focused attention on the role of women in society. Their stories span five centuries: Alice Arden (1550s), Mary Edmondson (1780s), Lizzie Borden (1890s), Ruth Snyder (1920s), Francine Hughes (1970s), and Louise Woodward (1990s). The dramatic representations of these women's trials are read in the context of other historical representations of female criminality, such as legal records, press coverage, ballads, and biography. This intertextual reading across disciplines and representations reveals the play script or screenplay and its production as an historical document; the dramatic representation of the criminal woman then emerges as one commentary among several on a particular trial and on the legal position encoded in that trial's verdict.

As we travel through the centuries, from Medea to Alice Arden to the more recent trial of Louise Woodward, the primary means of communicating the morality tales of women's crime changes. For narrative containment to be effective it must reach a broad section of the population. In sixteenth-century England, where this study begins, the primary means of cultural communication in the largely illiterate population was through ballads sung in the streets and plays performed in the public theaters. In the United States in the nineteenth and early twentieth centuries, before the advent of film and television, the public regularly attended the theater in both small towns and large cities. Now, the television has replaced the ballad and the theater as the primary means of communication.

Methodology

Each chapter begins with an overview of the legal and social position of women at the time the murder was committed, providing specific data on female crime rates as well as contemporaneous theories of female criminology. Then, each chapter focuses in depth on a particular case in which a woman was accused of murdering a member of her own family or, in one case, a child in her care. By analyzing the legal and journalistic discourse, comparing trial records and the public interpretations of those proceedings, I expose the ideologies of gender at work in the woman's trial. Finally, each chapter analyzes a play, movie, or television program that provides a dramatic representation of that woman's crime, trial, and punishment. By examining the ways in which the woman's story is formed into a morality play that warns other women of the dangers of self-determination, I place the dramatic representation into a broader circulation of gender instruction within the culture. Examining the ways in which women's legal status has evolved over five centuries reveals how representations of criminal women have reinforced traditional gender roles far more often than they have challenged them.

Traditionally, the legal subject has been a male subject, and as Catherine MacKinnon writes in *Toward a Feminist Theory of the State*, "The law sees and treats women the way that men see and treat women. The state authoritatively constitutes the social order in the interest of men as a gender."[16] In criminal law and its administration, the organization of gender is particularly visible. The law is written from the standard of the "reasonable man." This abstract rights-bearing person is embodied in male form.[17] Economic status, political affiliation, religious orientation, psychological history, and of course gender, quickly problematize the concept of one quantifiable reasonable standard of action and thought.

In any legal action, the accused is said to be represented by counsel; in a sense it is the *representation* of the defendant that the jury finds guilty or innocent. The representation does not negate the materiality of the defendant or the victim(s), but because the jury did not see the crime, it must be re-presented. The belief that the representation of the defendant as presented by counsel is the unmediated narration of "true" character is intensified if, like most of the women in this book, the defendant does not testify on her own behalf.

Until very recently women's experiences and perspectives were not incorporated in legal practice. Their stories have been told by men to men, and they have been judged according to the standards set by other "reasonable men." As a feminist historian I attempt to uncover the cultural construction of gendered identities and reveal how, historically, they have affected the outcomes of trials in which women are the accused. How and by whom was the woman described in court, in print, and on stage? What level of feminist resistance was present in her culture at the time of her trial or at the time of the representation of her crime in dramatic form? What standard of femininity was the woman being held against? How did her race, physical appearance, sexuality, marital status, economic position, or political beliefs affect her conviction or acquittal? How did they affect her historical and dramatic representation?

In "History as Usual?: Feminism and the 'New Historicism'" Judith Newton argues that it has always been a feminist project to focus on the cultural force of representation. Given the absence of women in official documentation, a "cross cultural montage," or interdisciplinary reading of multiple texts against each other, is the primary modus operandi for the recovery of women's history. But she argues that the texts that are read against each other are often productions of the same dominant culture that feminist historians have been attempting to read past.[18] As I focus on the representation of female criminality, I run headlong into Newton's concern. I have no trouble reading intertextually, for criminology is a highly documented field, but the documents I am drawn to—the legal, medical, criminological, journalistic, and dramatic—are almost exclusively authored by men. However, more problematic than the question of authorship are the gendered assumptions built into the legal and scientific community themselves. These assumptions, in addition to the strict conventions of the pre-twentieth-century stage, converge to obscure the self-representation of the female who is perceived by her culture as criminal. Tied as I am to the historically specific, gendered assumptions and values embedded in my source material, I have searched for feminine texts to read against the dominant narratives. Rarely do criminal or criminalized women leave a record of their own experiences or perspectives. Most either did not choose, or were not allowed, to testify at their own trials. However, the tension in absence is a motivation for a feminist, and I have attempted to animate my subjects' silence by looking at women's texts outside the theater and the law. Particularly useful in understanding the construction of gendered identities and their effects on women defendants are writings on marriage and childrearing, and texts of feminist resistance, such as suffrage and protest literature.

Each of the women in this study was the center of national attention in a sensational murder trial. Each became the subject of popular entertainment—in a ballad or a play or a television program—that kept her in the public psyche long after the jury delivered a verdict. Alice Arden's crime was still being played in public squares three hundred years after her body had burned to ashes. The longevity of these women's stories in a world where thousands kill and are killed in relative anonymity demands explanation.

Chapter 1, "Petty (T)reasons for Killing Her Lord and Master," focuses on the case of Alice Arden. Convicted and executed in the sixteenth century for the conflated crime of adultery and murder, Alice Arden begins this book because her story is the earliest extant dramatic narrative of domestic murder based on a documented historical event. The dramatic representations of

Alice Arden and the critical response to them reveal cultural anxieties about women in pursuit of economic independence, sexual self-determination, and self-governance in early modern England. Contained in the structured narratives of two plays and several ballads, the cultural reenactment of Alice's crime and its punishment attempts to justify the economic, social, and cultural restraints that for centuries subsumed a married woman in the legal persona of her husband.

Chapter 2, "Absence of (M)alice on the Victorian Stage," focuses on the nineteenth-century dramatic representation of Mary Edmondson. Hanged for the murder of her aunt in the eighteenth century, she was "rehabilitated" on the Victorian stage into an innocent woman, cut down from the gallows in the nick of time. The murderess presented the Victorians with a particularly vexing dilemma, for she had not only broken the law but she had, more problematically, violated the cultural code of womanhood. This chapter examines the defeminization of criminal women in medical, sociological, and criminological texts and the absence of the masculinized, criminal woman on the Victorian stage. By comparing the eighteenth-century trial of the real Mary Edmondson to the nineteenth-century dramatic retelling of her story, this chapter analyzes the role of the stage in the creation and perpetuation of the "angel in the house."

Chapter 3, "A Jury of Her Peers," focuses on the case of Ruth Snyder, a woman convicted of murdering her husband in 1927, and the representation of her story in Sophie Treadwell's expressionistic play *Machinal*. Depicted by the prosecutor and the press as a woman who posed a serious threat to the American way of life, Ruth Snyder was used as an example to those women who might take their new "freedom" too literally. In contrast to the press and prosecutors who represented Snyder as a deviant woman, an aberration far removed from the feminine ideal, Treadwell rejected the notion that femininity and criminal behavior are mutually exclusive and implied that any woman could find herself in Snyder's position. In *Machinal* Treadwell posits that a woman's natural state is not matrimony and motherhood but that those roles are forced upon her by a patriarchal culture that relies on female submission and self-sacrifice.

Chapter 4, "Totaled Women," examines the case of Francine Hughes, whose 1978 acquittal in the case of her husband's murder prompted one journalist to note that it was "open season on husbands." *The Burning Bed*, a television movie based on Hughes's case, aired as part of National Domestic Violence Week and was the first major movie about domestic violence to be broadcast on national television. Actress Farrah Fawcett, famous for her television role on *Charlie's Angels*, was cast as Francine Hughes; the television movie, viewed by over seventy-five million people, indelibly wedded the two women in the American psyche. The Francine Hughes created by Farrah Fawcett became for many the prototype of the battered wife, ironically reinforcing traditional notions of feminine passivity and self-sacrifice.

Chapter 5, "Medea Returns," examines the trial of British au pair Louise Woodward for the murder of eight-month-old Matthew Eappen, one of the two children in her care. It was a case closely followed by the media, broadcast "gavel to gavel" on *Court TV*, and later used as the inspiration for an episode of the popular legal television series *Law & Order*. The case was rife with ambiguity, from the coverage of the crime to the judge's eventual negation of the jury's verdict. Many of the themes that emerge in previous chapters are evident in the Woodward case—the equation of womanhood with motherhood, the idealization of feminine self-sacrifice, and the perceived danger to cultural stability represented by the mother who works outside of her home. Though these centuries-old conceptions of gender emerge in the Woodward case, they seem to have lost some of their traction; the unanimous chorus of hatred that greeted Ruth Snyder has devolved into a complex fugue of point and counterpoint. The case and its subsequent representations both embrace and resist the cultural desire to disassociate the idealized woman from the criminal and to criminalize the woman who steps outside traditional gender norms.

Chapter 6, "Narratives of Resistance," explores two contemporary plays that challenge the traditional narratives of containment usually applied to women who kill. Sharon Pollock's play *Blood Relations* offers a critique of patriarchal representation in the case of Lizzie Borden. Franca Rame and Dario Fo's *Medea* takes this icon of unnatural womanhood into the next millennium with a surprising justification for the murders. Both offer resistant feminist narratives that call the whole concept of "natural" womanhood into question.

Finally, a brief afterword looks at the recent case of Andrea Yates, a woman convicted of drowning her five children in order to save them from "being tormented by Satan."[19] As of this writing her story has yet to be dramatized, though one could certainly read the trial as drama. The Yates trial raises some provocative questions about the potential power of existing dramatic representations, in this case an episode of the television series *Law & Order*, to influence jurors and affect the outcome of a trial.

Dramatic representations of women who kill have played an important role in perpetuating notions of a "woman's place" and of what constitutes the very idea of woman herself. *Medea's Daughters* suggests that dramatic representations of accused women both drew upon and influenced legal and journalistic representations of criminal women. By examining these "popular entertainments" this book explores the intersection between the discourse of criminality, used to comment on women accused of legal transgressions, and the discourse of abnormality, used to criminalize women who transgressed traditional norms of femininity. By offering a resistant reading of these collective performances, my analysis aims to read "against the grain" and to offer the reader "the pleasure of resistance, of saying 'no': not to 'unsophisticated' enjoyment by ourselves and others, of culturally dominant images, but to the structures of power which ask us to consume them uncritically and in highly circumscribed ways."[20]

So let us begin with Alice. . . .

chapter 1

petty (t)reasons for killing her lord and master

By asserting her entitlement to grievance and self-will, and endeavoring to reshape her circumstances by means of violence, the murderous wife calls into question the legal conception of the wife as subsumed by her husband and largely incapable of legal or moral agency.[1]

BY ALL ACCOUNTS, Alice Arden of Faversham, in Kent,[2] conspired with her lover, the tailor Mosbie, to murder her husband, Thomas Arden, in 1551. There is no recorded plea of innocence, no documented testimony in her defense; the Faversham records simply state that Arden was stabbed to death in his own home on St. Valentine's Day and that Alice, Mosbie, and a host of conspirators were arrested, convicted, and executed shortly thereafter.

At a time when violence was not uncommon, Thomas Arden's murder merited a lengthy entry in Holinshed's *Chronicles of England, Scotland and Wales* (1577) nearly thirty years after the event. Holinshed's decision to interrupt his writing of the history of Edward VI's reign in order to give a detailed account of the murder is a testament to the hold this narrative of petty treason had over its Renaissance audience. At the end of his account Holinshed reports that Arden's body was dragged into a field, where it miraculously left its imprint on the ground for two years after his death.

Alice Arden, convicted and executed for the conflated crime of adultery and murder, left an even deeper imprint on Renaissance culture. Her story begins this book because it is the earliest extant narrative of domestic murder based on a documented historical event. A tale told and retold by ballad singers, historians, and actors for more than a century, Alice Arden's story bears examination not simply for its primogeniture but for its resonance with our own time. In this early narrative we can trace the beginnings, both legal and social, of our own beliefs about female criminality. Contained in the structured narratives of plays and ballads, the cultural reenactment of her crime and its punishment can be seen as an attempt to mitigate fears of sedition and to justify the economic, social, and cultural restraints that, for centuries, subsumed a married woman in the legal persona of her husband.

Petty Treason

Treason was, by definition, a crime against authority, and men convicted of high treason for rebelling against the monarch faced a violent death of mutilation, disembowelment, and decapitation. A man convicted of petty treason for having murdered a master or superior officer died less violently than the high traitor, but this was little comfort at the end of the day, when his body was displayed hanging in chains, a vivid symbol of the death and decay that was the inevitable consequence of insubordination.

In 1352 killing one's husband was first distinguished from other types of murder and designated as treason.[3] At this time there was no distinction between high treason (violence against the monarch) and petty treason (violence against one's husband) though later the two crimes would be divided. Women convicted of petty treason were sentenced to the same punishment as those convicted of high treason, but because it was not seemly to display the female body in public, they were burned at the stake. As Francis Dolan writes, "In legal theory, then, if not always in practice, the punishment of female traitors collapsed the distinction between the two kinds of treason: for women these capital offenses were not only analogous but virtually the same."[4] For a woman contemplating violent resistance, there was no legal difference between her husband and her monarch.

The analogy between order in the domestic site and order in the monarchy is a common one in Renaissance thought. In this context any resistance to domestic stability and hierarchy represented a threat to social order on a much larger scale. In a homily entitled "Exhortation, Concerning Good Order and Obedience to Rulers and Magistrates" (1559) the writer equates the positions of monarch, master, father, and husband, and asserts their rightful claim to the obedience of their subordinates. The writer's "authority" is God, who he claims has created a perfect hierarchical order, an order that, when overthrown by rebellious subordinates, results in chaos:

> Almightye God hath created and appoynted all things, in heaven, earth and waters, in a mooste excellente and perfecte order. . . . Everye degre of people in theyr vocation, callying, and office hath appointed to them, theyr duety and order. Some are in hyghe degree, some in lowe, some kynges and prynces, Fathers and chyldren, husbandes and wives, riche and poore, and everyone have nede of other: So that in all thynges is to be lauded and

praysed the goodly order of God, wythoute the whiche, no house, no citie, no commonwealth can continue and indure or laste. For where there is no ryghte ordre, there reigneth all abuse, carnal libertie, enormitie, synne, and Babylonicall confusyon.[5]

Were these fears of "Babylonicall confusyon," justified? How violent was the Renaissance home? Any historical reconstruction of crime statistics is problematic, but it is especially difficult in a period from which so many records have been lost. In Renaissance England many acts that would outrage us today were not reported or even recognized as crimes. Wife beating, for example, was legal, and many problems of domestic violence were often left to be handled by the community in shaming rituals. Still, by examining the assize records of Essex County in the years 1559–1625, one can begin to extrapolate the possible prevalence of domestic homicide in this period.

Of all reported homicides, at least 13 percent involved the killing of one member of the family by another or through the agency of another (as when a spouse hired an assassin). On the evidence of the assize indictments, wives were the victims in almost three-quarters of the instances of marital killing. If, in fact, wives were far *less* likely to murder their husbands than to be murdered by them, what accounts for the popularity and longevity of Alice Arden and other petty treason narratives?

Catherine Belsey writes in *The Subject of Tragedy* that the existing historical evidence "gives no reason to believe that there was a major outbreak of women murdering their husbands in the sixteenth century. What it does suggest, however, is a widespread belief that they were likely to do so."[6] The Essex County records for the Elizabethan period reveal that no women were convicted of petty treason, but the records do list several cases of frightened husbands seeking the protection of the courts.[7]

Though at least two plays based on actual cases of petty treason exist today, *A Warning for Faire Women*[8] and *Arden of Faversham* (Thomas Dekker and Ben Johnson's tragedy *The Page of Plymouth* is not extant), I will focus on the Arden play, whose popularity is evidenced by its three publications (1592, 1599, and 1633) as well as by its continued presence in our contemporary repertory. Though I will discuss the anonymous *Warning for Faire Women* later in the chapter, the petty traitor Alice Arden speaks most directly to the construction of the criminal woman in Renaissance drama. Imagined by ballad singers, historians, and playwrights and embodied by male actors, "Alice Arden" evolved into a complex text of discontented Renaissance womanhood, as created and performed by Renaissance men.

To better understand the dramatic construction of Alice Arden, it is helpful to trace the evolution of her story from the always elusive physical event, through the legal notes in the Faversham town records (*Wardmote Book of Faversham*), to the postexecution historical record (Holinshed's *Chronicles*), and finally into the ballads and play constructed for public entertainment and education. Each successive author retells the story of the crime, and each intervention allows us to see the way that the actual Alice was formed and performed until she was re-formed into a cultural icon of subversive womanhood.

The introduction to M. L. Wine's edition of *The Tragedy of Master Arden of Faversham*, published in 1973, contains extensive source material on both the historical event of Arden's murder and the stage history of the play. In a series of appendices to the play, Wine includes the official report of the Arden murder from the Wardmote book; the "historical" account printed in Holinshed's *Chronicles*; and also a 1633 ballad, presumably based on the anonymous play entitled "The Complaint and Lamentation of Mistress Arden of Faversham." It is from the Holinshed material and the Wardmote book that I draw what I will refer to as the "historical narrative" of the murder. I believe, with H. Aram Veeser, that "no discourse, imaginative or archival, gives access to unchanging truths."[9] Those sources claiming the authenticity of historical documents are intricately interwoven with the fictional and dramatic narratives; they too are stories, told from the point of view of those in authority, and as such must be read with a sensitivity to absent voices. For example, when we examine the legal record of the trial, it is important to remember that, at the end of the sixteenth century, the accused was not allowed counsel, and hearsay was routinely entered as evidence. The official story of Alice Arden and her conspirators comes to us through what Carlo Ginzburg describes as the often "hostile testimonies, originating from and filtered by the legal process that criminalized and executed them." In such affidavits, "the voices of the accused reach us strangled, altered, distorted; in many cases, they haven't reached us at all."[10]

Historical Narrative

Thomas Arden[11] was a wealthy customs official in Faversham, Kent, a position he had been appointed to by his father-in-law, Sir Edward North. According to one account Alice Mirfyn, Sir Edward's stepdaughter, was twenty-eight years old when she married the fifty-six-year-old Arden.[12] Alice's lover, Mosbie, was Sir Edward's servant, and according to one source Alice "had had familiarities with Mosbie before she was married, which made her friends [relatives] desirous of marrying her with Arden."[13]

Sir Edward served as the chancellor of the Court of Augmentations, a court set up by Henry VIII to manage and redistribute property confiscated from the church. After the marriage, much of the Faversham Abbey lands, as well as a house built on the Abbey property, was deeded to Thomas Arden; there can be no doubt that he became rich from these church lands.[14] Arden's greed for property and his disregard for the welfare of former tenants on the land, a central theme in the play, seems to have some historical grounding.

The Wardmote book provides the only information we have written by those who lived at the time of Arden's death. It gives a brief account of the "facts" of the murder:

> Arden was murdered by Thomas Mosbie, tailor, late servant to Arden's father-in-law Sir Edward North.
>
> Arden "did well knowe and wilfully did permit" the affair between his wife and Mosbie.
>
> Alice procured her husband's death so she could marry Mosbie.
>
> Mosbie's sister Cecily, Arden's servants Michael and Elisabeth were "counsellors to the murder."
>
> John Greene, George Bradshaw and the painter William Blackborne were "abbettors to the murder."
>
> Loosebag and Blackwill were hired assassins paid to kill Arden.
>
> Arden was killed while playing "at tables" with Mosbie. Blackwill strangled him from behind, Mosbie hit him on the head with a heavy iron, then slit his throat.
>
> Blackwill dragged the body out of the house, received payment and left. The servants dragged the body into the field where it was discovered.[15]

Holinshed's version, printed in the *Chronicles of England, Scotland and Wales*, is far better known to scholars of the play, though Holinshed constructs a narrative that differs on several key points from the Faversham record. Because Holinshed's *Chronicles* is generally acknowledged as the source for the anonymous play, his "adjustments" to the official account are the first step (that we can trace) in the construction of Alice Arden as an icon of female insubordination and revolt.[16]

From the official account in the Wardmote book, we learn only that Alice procured the murder of her husband with the help of many accomplices. Holinshed places her more firmly at the center of the narrative. In the Wardmote book, Alice condones but does not participate in the murder of her husband. In Holinshed's *Chronicles* Alice is presented as the driving force behind the plans to murder Arden. As in the Wardmote book, Holinshed describes Black Will strangling Arden from behind and Mosbie hitting him on the head with a heavy iron. But at this point his narrative takes a dramatic twist. Thinking Arden dead, the murderers drag his body to the counting house, where Arden suddenly revives. At that point Black Will gives him a "great gash in the face, and so killed him out of hand."[17] After Arden is dead, Holinshed "records" that Alice came in and stabbed her husband seven or eight times in the chest. After the body is dragged away Holinshed reports that Alice had a dinner party and asked her daughter to play upon the virginals while she danced. It is also to Holinshed that we owe the account of Arden's body leaving its imprint in the ground for two years after his death. The actual murder of Thomas Arden is inaccessible to us, but with the translation from the court records to Holinshed's *Chronicles*, the nine accomplices cited in the Wardmote book fade into the background and the adulterous wife takes center stage.

The Dramatic Text

Holinshed's *Chronicles* (1577, second edition 1587) is generally recognized as the source for the anonymous play *The Tragedy of Master Arden of Faversham*. The first edition of the play was published in 1592, forty-one years after the murder, and it enjoyed at least three publications, the final appearing in 1633. Doubtless the murder also inspired numerous pamphlets, broadsides, and sermons that have since been lost; one ballad, "The Complaint and Lamentation of Mistress Arden of Faversham" (1633), survives, and it is most likely based upon the play.

The play sticks fairly closely to Holinshed's description of the events, although it too alters certain key points in the narrative. Alice's re-positioning to the center of the murder plot, first accomplished by Holinshed, is, if anything, intensified in the play. In keeping with Holinshed's interpretation the play locates the driving force behind the murder in Alice's sexual desire for Mosbie. Through her characterization as a dominant and domineering force, Alice is shown controlling others, compelling them to do her bidding. Though many participate in the murder, it is Alice's ungovernable passion that kills Arden. In the text of the title page, focus shifts away from the tragic body of Thomas Arden, to center on Alice, the disloyal, wanton wife. She is the wicked woman whose lust is insatiable, shameful, and unforgivable:

TRAGEDY OF M. ARDEN OF FAVERSHAM IN KENT.

Who was most Wickedlye murdered, by the means of his disloyall and wanton wyfe, who for the love she bore to one Mosbie,

hyred two desperate ruffians Blackwill and Shakebag *to kill him.*

Wherein is shewed the great Malice and Discimulation
of a wicked woman,

the unsatiable desire of

filthie lust

and the shamefull end

of all murderers.

In the first scene, Arden laments his wife's passion for Mosbie. His friend Franklin, an entirely fictional character who serves as the play's moral sounding board, replies, "Comfort thyself, sweet friend; it is not strange that women will be false and wavering."[18] Woman's falseness and duplicity are established as the norm in the very opening moments of the play, and Alice's character is spawned from the basic assumption that women are by nature faithless. The playwright wastes no time unveiling Alice's deceitfulness. In her first scene with Arden she assures him that her love is constant, but no sooner has he left the room than she wishes for his death:

> ALICE: O that some airy spirit
>   Would in the shape and likeness of a horse
>   Gallop with Arden 'cross the Ocean,
>   And throw him from his back into the waves!
>   Sweet Mosbie is the man that has my heart:
>   And he usurps it, having naught but this,
>   That I am tied to him by marriage.
>   Love is a God, and marriage is but words;
>   And therefore Mosbie's title is the best. (7)

Worshiping her passion as "a God," Alice justifies the elevation of her own sexual needs and desires above the vows of marriage. She makes a mockery of her marriage vows, declaring that her oath of loyalty and obedience was nothing but "words"—a dangerous notion for a society that relied on the power of words, particularly those of the Bible, to enforce the control of masters over servants and husbands over wives. In 1632, in *Lawes Resolution of Women's Rights*, a legal encyclopedia for women, Edmund Tilney (Queen Elizabeth's master of the revels) explains that the absence of women's civil rights in the culture was directly attributed to her association with the Fall. "Eve's sin is the reason of that which I touched before, that women have no voyce in Parliament, They make no Lawes, they consent to none, they abrogate none. All of them are understood as either married or to be married and their desires are subject to their husband."[19]

Alice's first attempt at murder, by way of poisoned broth, fails when Arden becomes suspicious of the taste. As she plans her second attempt, Mosbie resists and tells Alice that he will not be part of her plan to murder her husband:

> MOSBIE: I have sworn
>   Never hereafter to solicit thee,
>   Or, whilst he lives, once more importune thee.
> ALICE: Thou shalt not need, I will importune thee.
>   What? Shall an oath make thee forsake my love?
>   As if I have not sworn as much myself
>   And given my hand unto him in the church!
>   Tush Mosbie; oaths are words and words is wind
>   'Tis childishness to stand upon an oath. (16)

Here Alice is shown as a woman to whom loyalty, truth, and constancy mean nothing. Driven only by sexual desire for Mosbie, Alice's passion for her lover knows no restraint. While Arden is away she keeps Mosbie in the house, sleeps with him, and places him in Arden's seat at the head of the family table. In a gesture mocking the permanence of the marriage vow, Alice even gives Mosbie the ring Arden gave her on their wedding day.

Though eventually Mosbie agrees that Arden must be killed, it is not for love of Alice. Mosbie is primarily concerned with the monetary gain he will incur when Alice becomes his wife. But in the midst of fantasizing about his potential wealth and power, he realizes that Alice will be an untrustworthy companion. In this scene he asserts the Renaissance belief that a woman was literally subsumed into the legal and spiritual identity of her husband at the moment of marriage (hence he should be safe), but since Alice has violently rejected the role of *femme couvert*, she cannot be trusted:

> MOSBIE: Yet Mistress Arden lives; but she's myself,
> And holy Church rites make us two but one.
> But what for that? I may not trust you Alice:
> You have supplanted Arden for my sake,
> And will estirpen me to plant another.
> 'Tis fearful sleeping in a serpent's bed,
> And I will cleanly rid my hands of her. (37)

Once Alice had broken her vows of marriage with Arden, she cannot go back to a purer state. In Mosbie's imagination she has been transformed from a woman into a serpent, the classical image of evil that disrupted the paradise of connubial Eden. Alice is no longer the disruptive Eve: she has transmogrified into Satan himself.

In the murder scene the anonymous playwright alters key details that amplify Alice's guilt even more forcefully than Holinshed's "history." In agreement with both historical sources, Arden is first strangled from behind by Black Will, and in agreement with Holinshed, Mosbie then stabs Arden, who falls to the ground, wounded but still alive. But the most significant use of dramatic license in the play occurs when Alice delivers the deathblow by saying the following:

> ALICE: What! Groans thou? nay, then give me the weapon!
> Take this for hindering Mosbie's love and mine.
> (She stabs him)

In the Wardmote book Alice only hires the assassins, she does not participate in the actual murder. In the play she stabs her wounded husband and, as he lies dying, taunts him with her love for another man.

In the epilogue to the play, the fictional Franklin apologizes to the audience for the "naked tragedy, wherein no filed points are foisted in to make it gracious to the ear or eye; for simple truth is gracious enough, and needs no other points of glossing stuff" (71). Consciously distancing itself from fiction, framed with promises of truth in its title page and epilogue, the play, a clearly fictionalized account, feigns veracity. It would have its audiences believe the "dispassionate" Franklin's promises of truth, the whole truth, and nothing but the truth. But it is a revisionist tale, and its most symbolic revision is to place the murder weapon in Alice Arden's hand.

The cultural performance of Alice Arden as a morality tale asserts that a man who cannot control his wife will suffer at her hand. The next step in this analysis leads us from the plane of representation to the lived experience of Renaissance women. How does Alice Arden's crime intersect with the patriarchal ideology that exacts a very real influence on women's lives? Toward this end I return to the veiled figure of the *femme couvert* and the dramatic Alice Arden's rejection of that cultural role.

Coverture is a romantic euphemism for the principle of ownership. Men owned their wives as well as their wives' property and assets, and if the orderly transference of property was to be assured, then fidelity and chastity were essential components of wifely behavior. A woman's chastity ensured her husband that his heirs would be of his own body and that the patrilineal succession of titles and estates would not be jeopardized. In an era where land was jealously guarded and easily confiscated, the legitimacy of heirs assumed paramount importance. For this reason Alice's crime of adultery represented more than a moral transgression; by jeopardizing patrilineal succession it provoked dangerous economic consequences and threatened to usurp male control over the transference of names and property.

When Arden complains of his wife's infidelity, Franklin, the play's voice of reason, replies, "Gentle Arden, leave this sad lament. She will amend, and so your griefs will cease; Or else she'll die, and so your sorrows end" (30). Alice will repent or she will die; either way Arden's sorrows will end. That he might grieve for his wife's death is not imagined nor is the possibility that an "authentic" or important life will end when Alice dies. Alice's worthlessness as an individual is perhaps never clearer than in this passage, where the playwright, almost inadvertently, affirms that Alice exists only as a facilitator for her husband's happiness.

Anita Loomba writes, "In patriarchal criminology, female crime is sexual and female sexuality is itself potentially criminal."[20] So dangerous was the sexually active woman that many Renaissance marriage manuals cautioned against a husband's giving his wife sexual pleasure in the marriage bed, for fear it would increase her appetite beyond his ability to satisfy her.[21] The word "chastity" was applied to married women as well as virgins, implying that a wife should treat sexual relations with her husband as a necessary, but not pleasurable, means toward procreation and advancement to her natural role as mother. If women's chastity was guarded in order to insure the legitimacy of heirs, the need to maintain it went far beyond the marriage bed of the Renaissance woman. To preserve it she might well be denied access to education, public discourse, and even freedom of movement. "Rigorous training in this all important quality [chastity] dominated her education, and brought with it as safeguards bashfulness, passivity, and seclusion from experience. Any intellectual pursuit had to be rejected if it seemed to imperil chastity, and even the most liberal writers excluded certain branches of learning on this ground."[22] A woman's docility, far from being natural, was the result of training and restraint. To preserve her prized chastity, she was instructed not to travel outside of her home, nor speak with men other than her husband, nor express herself passionately on any subject. In the dramatic representation of the crime, Alice's adultery, recorded in the legal sources, is transformed quite literally on the stage into the fatal blow that assassinates Arden in his own home. Alice Arden is what all women could become if chastity is not enforced, and her transformation from woman into serpent, paralleling Eve's fall from grace, serves to exonerate those who imprison their wives inside domestic walls of silence by implying that those who do not will pay the ultimate price. If we analyze the popular (and long-running) performances of *Arden of Faversham* as enacted morality tale, participating in the cultural education of the populace, the lesson for Renaissance men becomes quite clear: husbands must control their wives.

Up to this point I have focused on the ways in which narratives of petty treason, such as *Arden of Faversham*, consciously reinforced existing power relations between men and women in Renaissance culture. Despite their ability to function as narrative containments of resistance, ballads occasionally would give a glimpse of a domestic situation so brutal that "treason" seemed the only sane response.

In her study on representations (ballads, pamphlets, and plays) of domestic violence in early modern England, Dolan found thirty-two accounts of wives who murdered their husbands and twenty accounts of husbands who murdered their wives.[23] What is most interesting about these figures is not the disproportionate representation of female crime but the distribution of the representations over the period. In the one hundred years between the murder of Thomas Arden and the execution of Charles I, there are only two extant narratives of husbands murdering their wives. But despite statistics that indicate there was no outbreak of petty treason at that time, twenty-eight of the extant accounts of murderous wives were published between 1550 and 1650.

Dolan posits that the actual occurrence of petty treason was not at issue; rather, it was the fear of insubordination, the suspicion that social controls might prove ineffective in protecting the empowered, that fueled the immense popularity of these narratives.[24] "The very need to define such a crime, and the fairly regular opportunities to see or read about the offenders who committed it, suggest the pervasive fear that wives and servants could and would rebel; they might not acquiesce to their subordination, which was achieved by a complex network of constraints and coercions, a network that could break down."[25] After the English Civil War and the execution of Charles I, representations of petty traitors ceased to circulate with their pre-war vehemence. Perhaps this is because "justifiable" resistance to tyranny had become more harmonious with contemporary political thought.

Only two extant ballads written before 1650 present the murder of a wife by her tyrannical husband. One tells of Henry Robson (1598), who mixed ratsbane and ground glass, wrapped it in mouton skin, and inserted the poisoned ground glass into his wife's vagina.[26] The other tells the tale of John Dilworth (1607), who, after hitting his wife over the head, built a fire and threw her in to burn. But after the collective "treasonous" execution of the "tyrant" Charles I in 1650, the figure of the petty tyrant, the abusive husband or master, began to appear more frequently in popular ballads. We get a glimpse of the violence endured by some Renaissance wives in several ballads concerning abusive husbands who are eventually killed by their wives. Each of these narratives presents the abused wife sympathetically, but in the end they cannot go so far as to excuse her violent resistance to abuse.

A Warning for Bad Wives (1678) tells the story of Sarah Elston, who testified that she did not intend to kill her husband but was holding out scissors to defend herself from his blows, when he fell upon them and died.[27] In a story reminiscent of many contemporary accounts of domestic homicide, *A Hellish Murder* (1688) recounts the tale of Mary Aubrey, a battered wife who waits until her husband is asleep before she kills him in a "kill or be killed" desperation. According to Henry Goodcole, a minister of Newgate prison, on the night of the murder Aubrey's husband had beaten her savagely and "attempted the Forcing of [her] to the most Unnatural of Villainies, and acted such a violence upon her Body in despite of all the Opposition she could make, as forc'd from her a great deal of blood." Later, as her husband lay sleeping beside her, Goodcole records Mary's thoughts. "What will become of me? What am I to do! Here am I Threatened to be Murder'd, and I have no way in the World to Deliver myself, but by beginning with him."[28] She strangled her husband while he slept.

Though each of these ballads acknowledges that there are limits to a husband's legitimate power over his wife, they unequivocally assert that a woman's violent response is "ultimately unjustifiable and destructive of the political order."[29] Though the ballads do provide a reason for a woman's violence against her husband other than simple lust for another man, they still hold her accountable for treason. In the end the petty tyrant is killed, the petty traitor is burned, and all is right with the world.

Though these ballads provide anecdotal evidence of domestic battery, we cannot read into them an acceptance of female violence when utilized in self-defense. The ballads of petty tyrants do not pardon the molested wife, despite apparent sympathy for her pain. In light of the legal and social acceptance of wife beating in early modern England, this is not surprising. The *Rules of Marriage* (1489) advised husbands of their rights and responsibilities as the moral head of the household. "If your wife is of a servile disposition and has a crude and shifty spirit, so that pleasant words have no effect, scold her sharply, bully and terrify her. And if this still doesn't work . . . take up a stick and beat her soundly, for it is better to punish the body and correct the soul than damage the soul and spare the body."[30]

Furthermore, there is a significant difference in the tales of male-on-female violence relating to the cause or root of the violent behavior. Whereas the narrative of the petty traitor, as exemplified by Alice Arden, warns that unless properly disciplined and restrained, *any* wife might prove a serpent in her husband's bed, the narratives of petty tyrants attempt to portray the murderous or excessively abusive husband as an aberration, a monster quite unlike actual, honorable husbands. Whereas women's crimes spring from a husband's inability to control a woman's inborn wickedness, the responsibility for the petty tyrant's actions is laid at the devil's door.

The anonymous *Yorkshire Tragedy*, based on the trial and execution of Mr. Walter Calverley for the murder of his two sons, depicts the protagonist, "Husband," as a man possessed by the devil, driven by an evil spirit to a dissolute life of gambling and debts. When he squanders his considerable fortune, he believes, in his demented state, that he must kill his children so that they will not grow up in poverty. He manages to kill two sons and wound his wife before he is arrested and miraculously gains his senses back in time to repent and beg forgiveness from his wife.

In the opening scene two servants discuss the husband's abusive behavior, acknowledging and literally making a joke of the domestic violence his wife endures:

> SAM: Why he's married beats his wife, and has two or three children by her.
> For you must note that any woman bears the more when she is beaten.[31]

Later, the husband, arguing with his wife, "spurns" (kicks) her, telling her he "will ever hold thee in contempt" unless she sells her dowry and gives everything she has to him so that he might spend her money on "those pleasures which I most affect" (62). Later, he pulls a dagger on her, crying, "Money, whore, money, or I'll—" and is stopped from killing her only by the entrance of a servant announcing a visitor. Temporarily safe, the wife exclaims, "Was ever wife so wretchedly beset . . . that which some women call great misery, would show but little here" (71).

After killing his two sons and wounding his wife, the husband throws a maidservant down the stairs and goes off in search of his youngest child, who is with a wet nurse:

HUSBAND: Are you gossiping, prating, sturdy quean?
    I'll break your clamour with your neck! Downstairs,
    Tumble, tumble, headlong *Throws her down.*
    So, the surest way to charm a woman's tongue
    Is break her neck. (79)

Arrested before he can kill the last child, the husband immediately repents and begs forgiveness from his wife, and here the paradoxical position of the Renaissance wife becomes most apparent. Rather than display anger toward the man who has stabbed her and, just moments ago, killed her two sons, the wife forgives him and promises to work for his release:

WIFE: Thou shouldst not, be assured, for these faults die
    If the law could forgive as soon as I. (91)

Though the husband is unabashedly presented as a violent man, the wife always attributes her husband's brutal behavior to a "vexed spirit" that has possessed his soul, and despite his abuses, her vows to love, honor, and obey are not shaken. When a friend tries to comfort her after his arrest by reminding her that she still has one babe left, she replies, "Dearer than all is my poor husband's life" (92). A *Yorkshire Tragedy*, along with the ballads narrating the fate of petty tyrants, indicates an awareness and condemnation of domestic abuse. Still, the wife's proper response is love and forgiveness, even when her violent husband murders her children and stabs her in the chest. His life, no matter how reproachful or abusive, must be dearer to her than her own.

    In light of these representations of spousal abuse, how are we to read the following scene in *Arden of Faversham* when Alice twists the narrative of petty tyranny, falsely accusing Arden of abuse in order to gain Greene's help in murdering Arden:

ALICE: Ah, Master Greene, be it spoken in secret here,
    I never live good day with him alone:
    When he's at home, then I have froward looks,
    Hard words and blows to mend the match withal;
    And though I might content as good a man,
    Yet doth he keep in every corner trulls;
    And when he's weary with his trugs at home,
    Then rides he straight to London; there, forsooth,
    He revels it among such filthy ones
    As counsels him to make away his wife.

> Thus live I daily in continual fear,
> In sorrow; so despairing of redress
> As every day I wish with hearty prayer
> That he or I were taken forth the world. (17)

Embedded in Alice's lie is the truth that some women did suffer at their husband's hands and did in fact live in continual fear for their lives; but this message is negated by the deceitful mouth of the messenger.

What are the implications of placing a false accusation at the center of Alice's murder plot? Does it simply serve to reinforce the characterization of Alice as a manipulative liar? Or can this scene be read as documenting Renaissance culture's conflicted response to domestic violence? We can agree with Greene that Arden's "abuse" is heinous, but we are justified in refusing any responsibility for its actual occurrence. In one sense, as the ballads of petty tyranny show, it doesn't really matter whether a woman lies about domestic abuse or not. If Alice had been telling the truth, and Arden had indeed threatened to kill her, she would still have no legal right to engage in violent resistance or even to kill him in self-defense.

In his analysis of the critical response to *Arden of Faversham* over the past four centuries, Wine observes that Alice Arden has been hailed as the most realistic stage villainess ever created:

> Realistic portraiture triumphs in Alice Arden. The critical praise of her has bordered on the extravagant invoking comparisons with Clytemnestra, Lady Macbeth, Phaedra, Anna Karenina, Emma Bovary, Lady Chatterley and Miss Julie among others. Thorndike expresses the feelings of many critics when he writes that the 'greatest merit of the play lies in the portrait of Alice Arden . . . incomparably the most lifelike evil woman up to this time depicted in the drama.'[32]

Besides questioning the "evilness" of characters such as Clytemnestra and Emma Bovary, I must ask what is so *real* about Alice Arden? Why is a woman, whose only motivation for murder lies in wanton lust, more authentic and believable than Mary Aubrey, who, lying bloodied in her bed, thought, "What will become of me? Here am I Threatened to be Murder'd, and I have no way in the World to Deliver myself, but by beginning with him." Renaissance ballads and pamphlets have preserved the stories of battered wives, confirming that, for centuries, despairing women have lashed out in self-defense and have, on rare and desperate occasions, killed the man who had made their lives a living hell. But these women disappear in Alice Arden's shadow. The echo of her cry as she stabs her husband, "Take this for hindering Mosbie's love and mine!" has resonated through the ages, assuring the anxious patriarch that if a woman has killed her husband, he can be sure it was for petty reasons.

Mrs. Arden Regrets . . .

Alice Arden did not fade away with the Renaissance; she survived well into the eighteenth century, her crime retold in a myriad of forms as various as a puppet show (1736) and a ballet at Saddler's Wells (1799). Perhaps the best-known eighteenth-century version of the Arden story is found in George Lillo's play *Arden of Feversham* (posthumously completed by John Hoadley in 1759), a romantic re-vision of the Renaissance murder drama that, though it retains the murder, completely alters the circumstances under which it was committed. Far from being a machiavellian adulteress, Lillo's protagonist is barely recognizable as the wanton, lustful Alice of old. Even her name has been changed: instead of plain English "Alice" she is rechristened "Alicia," which is resonant with distant Italianate romance.

Unlike the early Alice, who recoiled from the role of wife and mother, Lillo's Alicia is an adoring helpmate to her husband and a mother of two. Alicia wishes her husband no harm, and far from being the driving force behind the murder plot, is merely a reluctant accomplice to Mosbie, who is the true villain of the play. From the outset Lillo sets responsibility for the murder squarely on the shoulders of Mosbie, who in the opening lines of the play proclaims that he has already tried to kill Arden three times:

> MOSBIE: The morning's dark, and horrid as my purpose.
> Thrice have my snares been laid for Arden's life,
> And thrice hath he escaped. I am not safe:
> The living may revenge. Oh! could I win
> Alicia to conspire her husband's fall,
> Then might I say, security, thou'rt mine,
> And laugh at all to come.[33]

Mosbie evokes images of entrapment as he plots to lure Alicia into his murderous conspiracy. By having Mosbie say, "Oh! could I win Alicia to conspire her husband's fall," Lillo establishes that, unprovoked, Alicia would not dream of doing harm to her husband or resisting her "natural" role as the subordinate wife. In the sixteenth- and seventeenth-century representations, Alice controlled her Mosbie, manipulating him with promises of sexual favors and monetary gain. Inherently evil, she had power and the strength of will to exercise it. In the eighteenth century,

Alicia, no longer sexually aggressive, is constructed as a pawn in Mosbie's master scheme.

Lillo suggests that Alicia was seduced by Mosbie in her youth (before her marriage) and that he who had "robbed [her] of [her] fame and virtue" used that secret to compel her obedience. Alicia does not encourage Mosbie's desire, and in fact is so dismayed by her infidelity that she asks to be killed for dishonoring her husband. Though Lillo may implicate Mosbie in Alicia's ruin, she fully accepts the blame for her own soiled reputation. This is a crucial difference between the earlier representations of Alice, in which the adulteress was shown actively resisting the societal roles assigned to her. Unlike her predecessor, who was determined to reclaim agency in her domestic sphere, Alicia mourns her inability to conform to feminine standards she believes to be just:

> ALICIA: Chaste matrons, modest maids, and virtuous wives,
>   Scorning a weakness which they never knew,
>   Shall blush, with indignation, at my name! (522)

Though Alicia resists at first, Mosbie ultimately convinces her to help him murder Arden. Alicia is sent into her husband's room to stab him while he sleeps, but looking on his face she cannot bring herself to harm him. Invoking the "powers" that guard the nuptial bed, she turns the knife on herself; with this suicidal gesture she upholds the sanctity of marriage with all its attendant constraints and fiercely resists the lure of insubordination:

> ALICIA: In thy own bosom plunge the fatal steel,
>   Or his, who robbed thee of thy fame and virtue.
>   It will not be—Fear holds my dastard hand:
>   Those chaster powers, that guard the nuptial bed
>   From foul pollution, and the hand from blood,
>   Have left their charge, and I am lost forever. (526)

Alicia, convinced that betraying her marriage vows has made her impure and monstrous, much to her surprise finds a forgiving lord in Arden. His willingness to welcome her back into the marriage bed purifies her "polluted" body and reaffirms her desire to be a loyal and faithful wife:

> ALICIA: The wandering fires that have so long misled me,
>   Are now extinguished, and my heart is Arden's.
>   The flowery path of innocence and peace
>   Shines bright before, and I shall stray no longer.

Unfortunately for the reconciled pair, Mosbie has drawn another plan to murder Arden with the help of the servants and two ruffians (Shakebag and Black Will). From this point on Lillo makes it quite clear that Alicia has no intention of assisting in the murder and in fact desperately wants to prevent it by warning Arden. She is unable to protect her husband when Mosbie sets her servant Michael to stand guard over her lest she betray them all.

The actual murder is quite similar to the historical and previous dramatic versions of the Arden case. Arden is attacked while playing backgammon with Mosbie. Black Will throws the scarf over Arden's head in order to strangle him, and a fight ensues. Though the murder scene begins in the traditional manner, it soon takes on a very different tone. Arden breaks free from Black Will, takes Shakebag's dagger, and defends himself with the help of his loyal wife, who encourages him and prays for his safety. Alice may have wielded a dagger—Alicia would take the deathblow for her husband if she could. When Mosbie finally pins Arden's arms, allowing the others to kill him, Alicia rushes to her husband's side. Holding the dead Arden in her arms, she begs to be forgiven and reaffirms her eternal devotion to her lord and master:

> ALICE: Turn not from me:
> Behold me, pity me, survey my sorrows!
> I, who despised the duty of a wife,
> Will be thy slave. Spit on me, spurn me, sir,
> I'll love thee still.
> MOSBIE: Mad fool, he's dead, and hears thee not.
> ALICE: 'Tis false—
> He smiles upon me and applauds my vengeance. (535)

With that, she snatches a dagger and strikes at Mosbie, then faints at his feet. When the mayor enters and charges Alicia with Arden's murder, she does not protest but declares that she "adores the unerring hand of justice."

We might well ask, Where is the Alice of old, the dangerous wanton, the passionate adulteress? Clearly Alice doesn't live here anymore. In her place is Alicia, a pale reflection of her defiant ancestress, who seems to resist rebellion as fiercely as Alice fought for control. Alicia does not question the inferiority of her position, only her own failure to fulfill expectations she deems just and natural. Until she is redeemed by her husband's forgiveness, Alicia can only see herself as a monster, a deviant woman unable to be the chaste wife and mother she longs to be. Lillo's whitewashing of Alice Arden heralds the birth of the Victorian stage heroine: not nearly as plucky, not yet able to resist—temptation, and fully embracing the role she has been given to play.

chapter 2

absence of (m)alice on the victorian stage

> In their own time the lady killers of the Victorian era, whether excused or vilified, were almost never presented as the women they were. They assumed multiple identities fashioned both by themselves and by others. In legal proceedings the masks they wore proved useful to them in some cases and detrimental in others, but in all, they served to shield contemporaries from the disturbing countenances of real women.[1]

THERE IS NO shortage of criminological, scientific, legal, and medical discourse on the cause and effect of criminal behavior in women during the nineteenth century. The works of Havelock Ellis, William Acton, Cesare Lombroso, and Luke Owen Pike illustrate the Victorian compulsion to decipher and control the deviant woman. Conversely, no other period has so clearly articulated the characteristics and qualities of the "good" woman as Victorian-era Britain. For all the political and scientific discourse on gender in Victorian culture, the Victorian stage showed little evidence of the cultural struggle to clarify gender expectations and to contain and control those men and women who eluded them. This chapter will examine the absence of the woman who kills on the Victorian stage, and through that absence attempt to understand how the theater participated in the construction of both the ideal and the criminal woman.

Though "fallen women" can be found in many popular melodramas of the period, women who committed crimes that might actually be tried in a court of law were rarely represented on stage. Although some of the popular highwaymen plays (most notably *Jack Sheppard*) starred actresses in trouser roles, in the theater women were the victims of crimes, not the perpetrators. While the fallen woman, or the adventuress as she was sometimes called, may have been the epitome of female sexual corruption, the melodramatic heroine symbolized idealized womanhood and as such was incapable of violent or criminal behavior.

Satire can often provide a more penetrating view of a theatrical phenomenon than traditional sources such as scripts, reviews, and memoirs. Nineteenth-century humorist and actor Jerome K. Jerome describes how the two diametrically opposed images of womanhood, the heroine and the villainess, were embodied on the Victorian stage. He admits to being rather bored with the heroine, whose constant state of crisis causes her to "weep a great deal":

> She is very good, is the Stage heroine. The comic man expresses the belief that she is a born angel . . .
> "Oh no," she says (sadly of course), "I have many faults."
> We rather wish that she would show them a little more. Her excessive goodness seems somehow to pall on us. Our only consolation, while watching her, is that there are not that many good women off the stage. Life is bad enough, as it is; if there were many women, in real life, as good as the Stage heroine, it would be unbearable.[2]

Jerome finds the adventuress far more appealing. She "sits on tables and smokes cigarettes" and never demands to be "unhanded."[3] Though he is being decidedly ironic, Jerome's description of the adventuress makes it clear that she is the antithesis of the loving wife and mother. He even jokes about her casual commission of infanticide:

> There is a good deal to be said in favor of the Adventuress. True, she possesses rather too much sarcasm and repartee to make things quite agreeable round the domestic hearth . . . ; but, taken on the whole she is decidedly attractive. She has grit and go in her. She is alive. She can do something to help herself besides calling for "George." She has not got a Stage child— if she ever had one, she has left it on someone else's doorstep, which, presuming there was no water handy to drown it in, seems to be about the most sensible thing she could have done with it.[4]

Jerome makes another observation that is very telling; he declares that the adventuress "is generally of foreign extraction. They do not make bad women in England, the article is entirely of continental manufacture and has to be imported."[5]

With Jerome's satiric image in my mind, in this chapter I examine why Victorian society was so invested in the belief that "they do not make bad women in England" and how, when real English women did commit crimes, the stage either ignored them or reformed them. As a case in point we'll look at the dramatic life, death, and rebirth of Mary Edmondson, a young woman executed at Tyburn in 1759 for the murder of her aunt. Like that of Alice Arden, her story was later dramatized and performed for the entertainment and edification of a middle-class audience. But unlike Alice Arden, who was one of many real-life women whose crimes were reenacted in ballads and plays, Mary Edmondson was the only living British murderess to be directly represented on the commercial London stage during the nineteenth century.

British playwrights often turned to true crime stories for source material; some notable criminals who were popular on the Victorian stage include Dick Turpin, Robert Macaire, Jack Sheppard, Jonathon Wild, Sixteen String Jack, Guy Fawkes, Paul Clifford, and Claude Duval.[6] Despite the popularity of male criminals, I am aware of only three nineteenth-century British plays that portray real women who had been accused of murdering a member of their own family. Of these three protagonists, two were foreigners and as such were sufficiently "different" from the audience members' own wives and daughters. The fifteenth-century Italian Lucretia Borgia, an alleged poisoner, was a popular stage villainess and appeared in many incarnations. A French woman, Marie LaFarge, was convicted of poisoning her husband and provided the basis for the Adelphi Theatre's *Lafarge; or, Self-Will in Women*. The only convicted British murderess represented on the Victorian stage was Mary Edmondson. Though she was undoubtedly British born, she was also separated from her audience by over one hundred years, and as we shall see, the dramatic representation of her crime is so severely altered as to be nearly unrecognizable.

As with Alice, to fully understand the implications of Mary's crime and punishment we first need a brief overview of the idealized Victorian woman and the "Angel in the House." Though 15 percent of British women reached their fiftieth birthday having never wed,[7] the idealized Victorian woman was Coventry Patmore's "Angel in the House," who in "a rapture of submission" gladly sequestered herself in the home while her husband spoke and acted for her in the public world.[8]

Patmore's celebrated poem extols the virtue of separate sexual spheres, a notion central to Victorian gender relations. According to this doctrine, women were to live inside the home, overseeing household matters in a comfortable cult of domesticity. There they would raise the children and create a nurturing space for their husbands, who in return toiled for the family's welfare in the outside world of work and politics. Though coverture still erased a wife's legal identity, the cult of domesticity invested her with an alternate self-image, a clearly defined role as the moral guardian of the home. But this new identity came at a high cost. By elevating the cultural status of a woman who performed the expected duties of wife and mother, the notion of separate spheres allowed men to justify the absence of women's rights in the public sphere.

The nineteenth-century married woman had few legal rights. Coverture still insured that not only did she lose her identity as a legal subject separate from her husband, she also forfeited all claim to any property she may have brought into the marriage. Despite the Victorian praise of motherhood, actual mothers had very few rights when it came to custody of their children. If a woman left a marriage for any reason, including abuse, she had no legitimate claim to her children, who were considered to be the legal property of her husband.

The punishment awaiting the woman who left her marriage could be seen on almost any given night on stage in one of the most popular dramas of the century, *East Lynne*. Isabel, the fallen woman who (for reasons that today would seem rather logical) abandons her husband and child, was a favorite role for leading actresses of the period; however, the popularity of the fallen woman on stage should not be interpreted as a willingness on the part of Victorian audiences to accept alternate standards of acceptable feminine behavior. Isabel does not offer a model of resistance to the Victorian woman but rather reinforces gender prescriptions by showing the devastating effects of leaving the domestic sphere. Disgraced and living in sin with the man who lures her from her marriage, Isabel warns other women not to make the mistakes she has made. This speech, recited thousands of times upon the Victorian stage, can be read as a virtual manifesto for wifely subservience:

> ISABEL: Alas! what is to be the end of my sufferings? How much longer can I bear this torture of mind, this never-dying anguish of soul? From what a dream have I awakened! O lady, wife, mother! whatever trials may be the lot of your married life, though they may magnify themselves to your crushed spirit as beyond the nature, the endurance of woman to bear, yet resolve to bear them. Fall down on your knees and pray for patience; pray for strength to resist that demon who would tempt you to accept them. Bear them unto death rather than forget your good name and your good conscience. Oh! I have sacrificed husband, home, children, friends, and all that make life of value to woman — and for what? To be forever an outcast from society, to never again know a moment's peace. Oh! that I could die and end my suffering and misery.[9]

Fallen women like Isabel posed no threat to the ideological construct of the natural wife and mother. For onstage, at least, these women always repented and, like Isabel, warned other rebellious women not to stray from the path of wifely virtue. These fallen women could titillate without threatening the stability of the Victorian home, for they always died (either by their own hand or by the ravages of grief and guilt), essentially proving that a woman who is not a wife and mother might just as well be dead. Lying in her forgiving husband's arms, the fallen woman makes an obligatory speech of repentance before she dies. Thus is she reabsorbed into the cult of domesticity, and the Victorian construction of the ideal woman carries on unchallenged.

In addition to legal constraints, medical and religious discourses also exalted women as morally superior but intellectually, biologically, and psychologically inferior. The highly respected Dr. William Acton writes that women were biologically constructed to bear children and that intense intellectual activity would drain blood from their reproductive system, perhaps even causing cancer of the womb.[10] Not only could an education erode a woman's womb, it could rot her soul as well. In *History of Crime in England* (published 1873–1876) historian Luke Owen Pike writes, "it follows that, so far as crime is determined by external circumstances, every step made by a woman towards her independence is a step towards that precipice at the bottom of which lies a prison."[11] Pike effectively criminalized female independence by claiming that the more active and energetic a woman was the more apt she was to become a felon. By fashioning the ideal Victorian woman as an angel in the house, the culture implied that those women found roaming around outside had gone to the devil.

The Victorian Murderess

The angel in the house, exclusively adapted to housekeeping and childbearing, may have been the idealized woman of the era, but she was hardly natural. Between 1855 and 1874 women were charged with nearly 40 percent of the murders committed in England and over half were ultimately convicted.[12] If the fiction of "natural" female submission and passivity was to be maintained, women capable of lashing out with violence against those they were supposed to protect must somehow be accounted for or explained away. The murderous woman was living proof that women were not submissive and altruistic by nature, and this provided a conundrum for those who maintained the "rightness" of separate spheres.

The murderess presented the Victorians with a particularly vexing dilemma, for she had not only broken the law but she had, more problematically, violated the cultural code of womanhood. Most women accused of murder in this period had killed a member of their own family; this was an action virtually unexplainable if one accepted the culturally constructed notion of femininity in the Victorian age. In Victorian criminology the myth of the morally superior and politically inferior woman was maintained by espousing this simple but elegant solution: women are not capable of criminal behavior, so if a woman does commit a crime she is not really a woman.

In *Criminal Women*, Victorian sociologist M. E. Owen expressed the common belief that it was impossible for a woman to commit a criminal act and remain a woman in the true sense of the word:

> The man's nature may be said to be hardened, the woman's destroyed. Women of this stamp are generally so bold and unblushing in crime, so indifferent to right and wrong, so lost to all sense of shame, so destitute of the instincts of womanhood, that they may be more justly compared to wild beasts than to women. . . . Criminal women, as a class, are found to be more civilized than the savage, more degraded than the slave, less true to all natural and womanly instincts than the untutored squaw of a North American tribe.[13]

The murderess was denaturalized, distanced from the "real" wives and daughters of the empire by emphasizing all of her masculine (and non-European) qualities. The first attack on the criminal woman's femininity was often directed at her physical appearance. Many sociologists and physiognomists believed that criminal women possessed masculine characteristics, which clearly marked them as deviant. The most concise document on female criminal physiognomy in the nineteenth century is Cesare Lombroso's *Female Offender*, published in 1898. Though he claims to analyze only outward appearances, Lombroso inevitably bases his conclusions on cultural beliefs about what is or is not "feminine." His theories are surrounded by charts, measurements, percentages, and photographs all verifying the scientific "authenticity" of his gendered assumptions.[14] To the criminal woman Lombroso attributes, to varying degrees, small stature, above-average weight, inferior cranial capacity, receding forehead, enormous lower jaw, projecting cheekbones, projecting ears, anomalous teeth, hairy moles, a deep voice, dark hair (with a tendency toward early grayness), dark eyes, and premature baldness. He adds that "the female assassin has most often a virile and Mongolian type of face."[15]

Lombroso concluded that women who had been convicted of murdering their husbands were "striking examples of having the bodies of women, but all the air of brutal men: whom they resemble sometimes, even in their dress."[16] In his pseudoscience any woman who does not appear or act sufficiently feminine is endowed with a criminal nature.

Older women, masculine women, and unattractive women—all possess criminal physiognomy in Lombrosian categories. Their masculine qualities (deep voices and hairy bodies) are outer proof of their polluted inner nature. Their feminine purity has been diluted with the atavistic qualities of non-European men.

One cannot separate the pseudoscience of criminal physiognomy from the ideological frame that produced it. Rather than creating the idea of assigning criminal characteristics to "masculine" women, the physiognomists were simply codifying the prejudices and fears of their culture. Even the discourse of sociology, which claimed to offer a dispassionate, scientific view of societal relations, was unable to distinguish documented fact from cultural beliefs. In his book on criminology, Victorian social theorist Havelock Ellis calls upon traditional wisdom to support his assertion that all criminal women possessed masculine attributes: "I have already frequently had occasion to note approximation of criminal women in physical character to ordinary men. *This has always been more or less carefully recorded in popular proverbs* and in the records of criminal trials" (emphasis mine).[17]

A positivist, Ellis is reluctant to claim that women's passivity and high moral nature are God given, and so by using the theories of Charles Darwin, he is able to explain, "scientifically," why women are less criminal than men. He begins by equating an "unfeminine" appearance with a criminal and degenerate nature, and then claims that unattractive women do not marry or reproduce and therefore do not pass on their criminal natures to future generations. "Masculine, unsexed, ugly, abnormal women—the woman that is, most strongly marked with the signs of degeneration, and therefore the tendency to criminality—would be to a large extent passed by in the choice of a mate, and would tend to be eliminated."[18]

Sometimes social theorists like Ellis had to go to ridiculous lengths to make reality correspond to their scientific maxims. In the same essay on female criminality, Ellis describes the case of a young woman who was executed in Paris for robbing and then murdering her lovers. He has to admit, far from looking "mannish" she was attractive and possessed of "sweet and feminine manners." However, he proves her abnormality by showing that she possessed "remarkable muscular strength." Just in case her physical strength was not enough to defeminize her, Ellis adds that not only did she dress as a man but her "chief pleasure was to wrestle with men, and her favorite weapon was the hammer."[19]

Many crime historians have noted that nineteenth-century juries felt uncomfortable sentencing a woman to hang, and were often more lenient than they would be with a man accused of the same crime. "There was one circumstance that could overturn the normal pattern of leniency towards women in sentencing. This occurred when women broke the unspoken rules of gender and sex roles and acted 'mannishly,' aggressively, or without due deference. There was little chivalry displayed toward women who came within the ken of the courts and had broken social taboos."[20] If a woman was "womanly" enough it was easier to believe that no crime had been committed, but if she was "mannish" in behavior or appearance she faced certain conviction.

It is difficult to document the theater's participation in the masculinization of criminal women. Though sociologists, criminologists, and doctors were successfully defeminizing women who killed, the Victorian stage was subject to legal and social constraints that prevented dramatists from examining the complex nature of women who kill. The office of the Lord Chamberlain regularly denied licenses to plays that portrayed "questionable" characters, situations, or languages.[21] Though occasionally the representation of a murderess onstage was allowed by the Lord Chamberlain, the guilty woman was never to be portrayed sympathetically and she must suffer the appropriate punishment either in prison, in the madhouse, or in death.

Even if the Lord Chamberlain had permitted the sympathetic portrayal of a murderess on the stage, the producer would have been hard put to find an actress willing to play the role. In her study of the nineteenth-century actress as working woman, Tracy Davis discusses the actress's marginal social position and her need to lead an exemplary life both on the stage and off. The actress who portrayed a morally unacceptable or socially threatening character risked defaming her own character, as she became equated with the role she portrayed onstage. Davis writes that "the private selves of women who did not specialize in conventionally feminine roles, or who performed in illegitimate lines of business that contravened gestural and vestimentary social norms, were particularly subject to unflattering social judgments."[22] It does not seem surprising, therefore, that the conventions of the Victorian stage, steeped as they were in the culture that produced them, would not allow for the portrayal of a murderess, particularly one who had killed a member of her own family.

An example of the British public's conflicted view of the criminal woman on stage can be found in the response to the Adelphi Theatre's production of *Lafarge; or, Self-Will in Women*. The Lord Chamberlain received the following letter of protest about the performance via the *Morning Herald*: "If English audiences are to be thus brutalized under the 'express sanction' of the Chamberlain's office—if the popular mind is, in its recreations, to be familiarized with lust and murder—the sooner the House of Commons relieves your lordship of your present theatrical privilege the better."[23] The

Theatrical Journal responded in the play's defense, emphasizing the piece's usefulness as a morality tale, which could sway young wives (who might be tempted to emulate Madame Lafarge) back toward the path of virtue:

> Some stupid person thought proper to apply to the Lord Chamberlain to suppress the performance of it. It is now before the public and affords a splendid night's amusement, without injuring the morals of the rising generation; on the contrary, it is a lesson to those who might err through jealousy. *The dramatist . . . has thrown aside all the circumstances connected with the death of her husband and the subsequent trial of Madame Lafarge on the accusation of administering poison.*[24] (Emphasis mine)

What is fascinating about this defense of the play is the way in which the author disclaims *all* factual connection with the actual Madame Lafarge— the real circumstances have been "thrown aside" and replaced with a "lesson to those who might err." The fictionalized account of a woman who kills could be shaped by the author to provide a lesson to the women of the realm. The implication is that a real story, enacted as it occurred, was too unstable, too complex to function as a morality tale. In real life, good and evil are not always so distinct and justice is both relative and elusive.

Mary Edmondson

The custom of altering historical circumstances to fit a preconceived dramatic formula in which good would triumph over evil was standard practice on the Victorian stage. But the dramatization of Mary Edmondson offers us a rare look at the dramatic rehabilitation of the criminal woman. The real Mary Edmondson is an enigma; whether she was guilty or not we will never know, but she died proclaiming her innocence on the gallows. In the genre of criminal biography, the dramatic climax is always the criminal's tearful repentance at Tyburn, and contemporary accounts confirm that convicted criminals almost always asked forgiveness before their execution. But Mary Edmondson did not conform to type; she protested her innocence to the end, and in an ironic gesture she stood upon the gallows and forgave those who had helped to convict her.

Just as with the Arden narratives, the "facts" of the case are very hard to ascertain, as each recorder wove his own interpretation of the event into the historical evidence. As was the custom in the eighteenth century, Mary Edmondson's story was recorded in street pamphlets and criminal biographies. Lincoln Faller describes how these popular narratives regularly "fictionalized" their historic subjects: "Popular writers, and presumably their audiences, shaped the facts of actuality into patterns convenient (and useful) to their imaginations . . . facts were often invented and [the criminal's] individuality, variously compressed and expanded, was ultimately denied as they were absorbed into the myths of crime."[25]

The primary historical source for Mary Edmondson is the *Newgate Calendar*, an anecdotal record of convicted eighteenth-century criminals, based primarily on the sessions papers from the proceedings at the Old Bailey. The opening of Mary's account reads, "There is, and perhaps ever will remain, a mystery in the case of this convict. If she was guilty, she was one of the vilest of hypocrites; if not, the circumstances against her were so strong that the jury could scarcely avoid convicting her."[26]

The following series of events is the version of the crime recorded in the *Newgate Calendar* (1825). Mary Edmondson, the daughter of a Yorkshire farmer, had been sent to live with her widowed aunt, a Mrs. Walker, in Rotherhite, where she lived for two years "comporting herself in the most decent manner, and regularly attending the duties of religion." Late one evening Mary escorted a neighbor, who had been visiting Mrs. Walker, across the street to her home. Moments after Mary left the neighbor's house, an oyster seller noticed that Mrs. Walker's door was open and then heard Mary crying out, "Help! murder! they have killed my aunt!"

Mary ran next door to get help while several men from the pub went to investigate the murder scene. They found Mrs. Walker with her throat cut, lying on her right side with her head near a table that was covered with linen she had apparently been folding. Mary told one of the men, a Mr. Holloway, that four men had entered through the back door, one had grabbed her aunt from behind, and the other, dressed in black, swore that he would kill her if she uttered a sound. Mr. Holloway noticed that Mary's arm was cut, and when asked what had happened, she replied that one of the men had "jammed it with the door." Holloway did not believe her and accused Mary of murdering her aunt, at which point she "fell into a fit, and, being removed from a neighbor's house, was blooded by a surgeon, and continued there until the following day, when the coroner's inquest sat on the body, and brought in a verdict of willful murder; in consequence of which she was committed to prison."[27]

The case against Mary was constructed on purely circumstantial evidence: the cut on her arm, Mr. Holloway's initial suspicion, and perhaps most damning, the fact that items she said had been stolen by the intruders were found hidden underneath the privy floor along with a bloodstained apron. Though the author of the *Newgate Calendar* indicates that Mary offered a defense, he did not deem it necessary to record it, but writes only that "She made a defense indeed; but there was not enough probability in it to have any weight."²⁸ No official record of her defense remains. The author concedes that Mary was convicted "on evidence, which though acknowledged to be circumstantial, was such as, in general opinion, admitted little doubt of her guilt."²⁹ There must have been very little doubt indeed, for the jury returned its verdict in just under five minutes.

Mary continued to protest her innocence while she awaited her execution in Newgate prison, and many people believed her, including a prison clergyman who plead for a reprieve, but to no avail. Condemned on a Saturday, Mary was brought to the place of execution on the following Monday, where "she behaved devoutly" and left these final, troubling words: "It is now too late to trifle either with God or man. I solemnly declare that I am innocent of the crime laid to my charge. I am very easy in my mind, as I suffer with as much pleasure as if I was going to sleep. I freely forgive my prosecutors, and earnestly beg your prayers for my departing soul."³⁰

In a society that sought clarity and order from its legal code, Mary's death, without the required confession or repentance, was disturbing because it implied that either she was innocent or, by eighteenth-century standards, she was "inexplicable."³¹ What murderess facing her Maker in the moment of death would not confess? The only reasonable answer was that she was not guilty. However, the implication that the state had murdered an innocent girl was so unacceptable, that after her death criminal biographers reconstructed Mary's life story in order to, retroactively, establish her guilt beyond any reasonable doubt. Five different pamphlets appeared, published immediately after her execution. One spoke in Mary's defense and one, written by her brother-in-law, took a neutral position. The others set out to give Mary a criminal personality and a violent past, fabricating huge sections of "historical" biography to make her seemingly inexplicable crime comprehensible. Unless Mary could be explained as these accounts presented her—a representation that required at crucial points the support of fiction—then "from an eighteenth-century point of view, she could not be explained at all."³²

The biographers distort and even invent facts in order to create a Mary Edmondson who their readers could believe was capable of murder. One pamphlet records that Mary "could not bear to be rebuked" and that she once stabbed her mother in the stomach with a penknife. No other version mentions this, and it is vehemently denied by Mary's brother-in-law, Mr. Clarke, whose pamphlet is titled *Refutation*.³³ While other biographers claim that Mary's parents sent her away to live with her aunt because they feared her temper and violent nature, Clarke explains her servitude in her aunt's house in a very different way. He claims that Mary was engaged to be married to a clergyman and that her parents, "thinking her not so well qualified for a clergyman's wife as they could have desired," sent her to learn household skills at her widowed aunt's home in London.[34]

No other biography indicates that Mary was engaged to be married, and in fact several take great pains to discredit her femininity and wifely potential. One author writes that Mary was "naturally of a morose and haughty and stubborn Spirit." Another calls her "somewhat passionate, resolute and of a masculine Spirit." Still another claims that her parents felt she was "headstrong, self-willed, uncontrollable and unadvisable" and "very careless and indifferent about Household affairs."[35]

It is significant that the biographers who attempted to prove Mary's guilt frame her character as distinctly unfeminine, leaving the impression that Mary was not a very "womanly" woman. They assign her highly masculine attributes, even a "mannish" appearance, in order to locate her criminality in what are perceived as unwomanly, hence "unnatural," qualities of appearance and temperament. Still, for all their reconstructive historicizing, these biographers could not erase the vision of the young woman upon the gallows protesting her innocence to the end and forgiving those who were about to hang her.

One hundred years after her enigmatic death, Charles H. Hazelwood, drawn perhaps to the mystery that lingered around her case, resurrected Mary on the London stage. *Mary Edmonstone; A Pathetic and Romantic Drama* premiered at the Britannia Theatre in December 1862. Hazelwood's version of the story bears little resemblance to any of the historical narratives. True to the conventions of the nineteenth-century stage, Mary, as heroine of the piece, does not have any of the negative attributes assigned her by the "biographers." Hazelwood softens what they called unmanagableness into "high spiritedness," easily explained as the youthful energy of a country girl suddenly thrust into the big city of London. Clearly, Hazelwood also wishes to resolve the mystery of Mary's execution, but unlike the eighteenth-century biographers who "created" a criminal personality for Mary in order to explain away the doubt, he simply asserts that Mary did not confess to the crime because she did not do it.

In the first scene, Hazelwood presents Mary as a high-spirited girl, somewhat frivolous, but safely engaged to a local pastor. Her aunt, Mrs. Walker, complains to her servant that Mary's behavior is not suitable for a clergyman's wife:

> MRS. WALKER: I wish my niece Mary was as dutiful as you are Gregory. I sent for her from Yorkshire, thinking she would be a friend and companion for me, but the giddy girl's head seems completely turned since she has been in London; she'd be at some place of amusement every

night if she could, but I object to such frivolity. Being as she is, betrothed to Mr. Francis King, the clergyman, I am anxious she should follow my example, and set her face against vain pleasures of all kinds.[36]

The aunt, disapproving of Mary's irreverent sense of humor, threatens to place her niece in domestic service to ready her for marriage. It seems that Mary has only two options: to be a good housekeeper and wife or to learn the skills necessary for that "occupation" as a servant in someone else's house. The option of living on her own or enjoying the city life at her own leisure is completely out of the question. Gregory asks Mary why she hasn't become more serious since she became engaged:

> MARY: Can't one be merry and wise at the same time? Do you suppose that really kind-hearted people always pull a face a yard long, and are as stiff in their manners as a couple of deal boards. Not they; merry hearts make smiling faces; and where there is good humor you will mostly find good dispositions. (4)

These hardly seem the words of a "headstrong, self-willed, uncontrollable and unadvisable" murderess. Hazelwood's heroine is charming, kindhearted, and filled with good humor; though she gets frustrated with her cross aunt, she never offers serious rebellion. She never resists her domestic calling. Looking forward to her marriage with Francis, she longs for the day she can be a housekeeper in her own home.

While Mary is contemplating the freedom that marriage will bring her, her brother Mark appears. He is in debt to two ruffians and hopes to borrow money from his aunt, but Mary persuades him not to trouble the old woman. Mark then leaves (presumably to earn an honest living) but the two ruffians, having followed him to Mrs. Walker's house, rob and murder her. Since the audience has seen the murder enacted on stage, there is no mystery: the audience knows Mary is innocent. Unfortunately, for Mary, no one on stage does.

Mary returns to find her aunt's body and a bloody knife with the initials M. E. on the handle. Believing they stand for Mark Edmonstone (her brother) she tries to hide the knife. It is discovered, however, and the magistrate, thinking the M. E. stands for Mary Edmonstone, places her under arrest for murder. Mary does not speak in her own defense because she fears that her brother is guilty of the murder, and she is willing to sacrifice her own life before she will jeopardize his. When Mary refuses to answer the magistrate's questions, her fiancé, Francis, turns her silence into a crime against him. "Have you no thought for me, none—I who have toiled through poverty and difficulty to better my position—that I might also better yours." He calls her a "cruel, stubborn, wicked girl!" and pushes her to the ground as she tries to cling to him for protection (16). The first act ends with this tragic tableau.

Tried and sentenced to be executed, Mary discovers, too late, that her brother is innocent of the crime. He had lost his memory in a debtor's prison and had just that morning discovered that Mary is sentenced to hang for the murder of their aunt. At this point it is too late for Mary to change her story, and she castigates herself for believing her brother could have been capable of murder. Condemned to die for no reason at all now, Mary despairs: "I have played with existence as a child would with a toy, and now see it lying broken before me" (22).

But all is not lost. (When is it ever in Victorian melodrama?) Mark realizes that the two ruffians he owes money to are in the cell next door, sentenced to die for arson and robbery. Lo and behold, one of them is named Michael Evans, hence the incriminating M. E. on the knife handle. As Mary is led to the gallows, her brother pleads with the real criminals to confess: "It is not only her life, but mine that trembles in the balance; for never can I live to be pointed at as the brother of a murderess" (26). They refuse and the ballad singers are already selling Mary's "last dying speech and confession" on the street (a nice nod to the fictional histories created as a matter of course at the gallows site) when Michael Evans repents and confesses his crime to the prison governor. Mary is cut down from the gallows at the last moment and, barely conscious, is carried, alive but lifeless, drained of her former spirit, onto the stage for the final tableau.

At first it would seem that we could learn nothing about nineteenth-century female criminality from this highly constructed plot, primarily because in this version Mary is innocent. As in much nineteenth-century discourse, however, examining what is not said can often be as informative as analyzing what is. A strong articulation of gendered values emerges if you consider what the playwright did not include from the historical record left by Mary's "biographers." Hazelwood's Mary is neither mannish, self-willed, uncontrollable, or unadvisable, nor is she adverse to housework. Clearly, she fulfills nineteenth-century expectations of femininity. Noting which of the negative character traits assigned to Mary in the pamphlets Hazelwood ignored or transformed provides an excellent example of how a woman could be decriminalized for representation on the Victorian stage. Her initial high-spiritedness and frivolity, so evident in the first scene, are punished by the trial she endures, but because she is willing and eager to perform the loyal duties of sister and wife (she still loves Francis despite his immediate rejection of her) she will be redeemed in the end.

Mary becomes increasingly passive as the play progresses, dominating the first scene but then scripted into a position of silence and inaction. In the final tableau she lies, barely conscious, an innocent woman in her husband-to-be's strong arms. She can be saved but only at the expense of her individuality and spirit.

In Hazelwood's "pathetic and romantic drama" Mary is tamed by an act of self-sacrifice that transforms her from a "giddy" girl into a true Victorian woman. By placing the needs of others far above her own, even at the cost of her own life, Mary is absorbed into the comfortable gender expectations of an age that equated femininity with passivity and service to others. Her acceptance of womanly sacrifice, far more than her actual guiltlessness, is offered as proof of Mary's innocence.

Cultural anxiety coupled with conventions of the Victorian stage, and the dictates of the Lord Chamberlain's office, guaranteed that there would be no authentic representations of women who killed on the Victorian stage. In her study of Victorian murderesses, Mary Hartman calls the thirteen women she examines "uncomfortably ordinary," but Victorian culture and the theater it produced did everything in its power to shape the criminal woman as an aberration. If a woman's life story did not reinforce or support the cultural construction of gender, the choice was clear: ignore her or, as in the case of Mary Edmondson, change her story. It would be many more years before dramatists would begin to question the construction of femininity or to critique the culture that criminalized those who would not conform to its gender expectations.

The idea that virtue must always triumph on the stage was a common Victorian trope—but whose idea of virtuous behavior would it be? The men who wrote for the theater clearly believed it was virtuous for a woman to suffer without complaint and to have no thought for her own safety. True, if her brutish husband was not reformed by the wife's love, he would die in the end (either from alcoholism or while engaged in a criminal act) but the heroine stuck by him no matter what the cost to herself. The woman who takes the blame for a loved one's crime is a common character in the Victorian drama. As the mandatory death of the fallen woman demonstrated, these dramatists also believed that it was not virtuous for a woman to place her own happiness before that of her husband's. Remember the words of advice Isabel offers to other wives in *East Lynne*: "O lady, wife, mother! whatever trials may be the lot of your married life, though they may magnify themselves to your crushed spirit as beyond the nature, the endurance of woman to bear, yet resolve to bear them."[37]

Like the legal system, which provided virtually no adequate protection for abused wives, nineteenth-century playwrights espoused the grin-and-bear-it philosophy when it came to domestic violence. Parliament did not grant women the right to leave their abusive husbands until 1895, and neither did Victorian dramatists. Fallen women who had left their husbands and children, or virtuous heroines who stuck by their husbands through thick and thin were staples of the Victorian stage. The one character that never appeared was the woman who walked away from her family because she would have been beaten to death if she did not.

Domestic abuse presented the Victorians with a complex social dilemma, for it problematized the whole concept of coverture and separate sexual spheres. The justification for denying a wife legal rights was that her husband was supposed to protect her, but this left the abused wife with no recourse in the public realm if her husband was the one she needed protection from. John Stuart Mill, introducing the Woman's Suffrage Reform Bill in 1867, tried, unsuccessfully, to convince Parliament that police records showed women could not rely on men for protection. Mill charged that even when abusive husbands were convicted of assault, the penalties were so light as to be nothing but an inconvenience.[38]

The violent husband was occasionally represented on the Victorian stage, but he was inevitably of the lower class, usually a criminal, and probably foreign. Wives who resisted this violence were much harder to find; they preferred to stand by their man no matter what the cost to themselves or their children. On the whole Victorian dramatists shied away from presenting domestic violence. However, references to the common occurrence of violence in domestic situations can be found in other forms of popular culture. An extremely popular form of entertainment was *The Punch and Judy Show*, a favorite of children and adults alike. The violence in this puppet show was quite intense; in the course of a half-hour show Punch bashed his child's brain in, threw him out the window, and then beat his wife to death when she complained. This was all played for humor, and crowds howled with delight at the violent antics of the little "everyman." One observer had wondered whether Punch's violent method of extricating himself from a tiresome marriage might give some other unhappy husband murderous ideas:

> Sometimes I note a henpeck'd wight,
> Enjoying thy martial might,—
> To him a beatific *beau ideal*:
> He counts each crack on Judy's pate,
> Then homeward creeps to cogitate
> The differences 'twixt dramatic wives and real.[39]

In spite of the nonstop violence, *The Punch and Judy Show* was, for the most part, considered harmless entertainment suitable for all ages. In *Picturesque Sketches of London* (1852) Thomas Miller describes a small boy captivated by the puppet show: "Look at that ragged woman holding up her dirty child. The little rogue claps his tiny hands, and crows again at every blow Judy receives." Punch and Judy, found on any given day on East End street corners or in West End drawing rooms, indeed offered Victorians a morality tale, and the moral was this: He who has the stick wins.

Beneath the surface of the English cult of domesticity there emerged a deep current of agitation that threatened to expose the true nature of the Victorian home. In late-nineteenth-century England a rising suffrage movement began to challenge the exclusivity of a masculine legal code, and for the first time a small but dedicated group of men and women openly questioned the legitimacy of coverture as a philosophical and legal convention. Although women did not legally attain "full personhood" in marriage until 1895 (with the Summary Jurisdiction Act, which allowed a woman to leave her husband for "persistent cruelty"), a series of legal decisions including the Divorce Act (1857), the Married Women's Property Acts (1870, 1882), and the Matrimonial Causes Act (1878) significantly challenged the legal precedent of coverture.

As women acquired more rights, representations of the female offender in the courts, press, physiognomical handbooks, and on the stage became enmeshed in a larger anxiety about feminist emancipation. Women who usurped what the culture had coded as masculine attributes and rights—sexual freedom, political activism, economic independence—found themselves criminalized, while those who had actually committed a crime were stripped of their femaleness. The criminal woman was so intensely vilified because her very presence in the culture exposed the fragility of the Victorian construct of femininity.

Arsenic and Old Men

By the late nineteenth century traditional explanations of female criminality came under pressure from social reformers and feminists. The idea that women were led to murder by their unbridled sexuality or their unnatural masculine qualities persevered, but the gnawing sense that there might be other, more complex, reasons for the prevalence of domestic murder was lurking in the wings. Havelock Ellis concludes his study of the British criminal with this caveat: "To kill the criminal is never satisfactory, because we do not kill his accomplices, bad social conditions and defective institutions;

we leave untouched the false social sentiments that urged the unmarried girl to kill her own child, or the rigid marriage system that made it easier for the man to kill his wife than to leave her or to allow her of leaving him."[40]

Many feminists believed that alternate explanations for female criminality—economic and physical dependence, impossible divorce legislation, alcoholism, and abuse—would never be reflected in the judicial process until women were judged by a jury of their peers, a jury of women. Nineteenth-century feminist Elizabeth Wolstenholme-Elmy expressed the view of many nineteenth-century feminists when she wrote, "Women have never in the case of a criminal trial the protection of a jury of their peers—they are prosecuted or defended by men, tried by men, judged by men. Is it impossible that sex bias should ever work injustice? Does it not at the very least, often lead to the forgetfulness or neglect of the most important considerations?"[41]

At the end of the nineteenth century Florence Maybrick was tried for the murder of her husband. Mr. James Maybrick, like many Victorian gentlemen, was addicted to arsenic, which could be taken in small doses as a "pick-me-up."[42] Given Maybrick's years of habitual "arsenic eating," Florence's lawyers argued that his death was caused by a self-induced overdose and not a deliberate poisoning by his wife. James Maybrick was an acknowledged hypochondriac; when he died, over one hundred bottles of medicine were found in his home and twenty-eight more in his office. Also found in the house were many boxes filled with packages of arsenic, enough to kill more than fifty healthy people.[43] In addition twelve sheets of flypaper (laced with arsenic) were found; they had been purchased by Florence Maybrick, ostensibly as a cosmetic aid.

In the course of the trial it came out that Florence and James had quarreled shortly before his death and that she threatened to leave him after he had given her a black eye. According to a maid's testimony, James tore his wife's clothes and told her that if she left she would never see the children again. The maid begged Mrs. Maybrick to stay "for the sake of the children."[44]

Medical experts argued about whether the quantity of arsenic found in Maybrick's body was capable of killing him. Their contradictory evidence bolstered Florence's case, and she enjoyed significant public support until she made the fatal error of confessing to adultery in her statement to the court. Florence's admission of adultery turned judge and jury against her, though no one seemed disturbed by James Maybrick's longtime extramarital affair. If anything it was seen as a motive for Florence's "revenge." Justice Stephens, who was recovering from a recent stroke, cited Florence's love letters as evidence of a murderous intent:

She, while her husband lived and, according to her own account, while his life was trembling in the balance—even at that awful moment there arose in her heart and flowed from her pen various terms of endearment to a man with whom she behaved so disgracefully. That was an awful thing to think of, and a thing you will have to consider in asking yourselves whether she is guilty or not guilty.[45]

Within half an hour Florence was found guilty and sentenced to death. Asked if she had anything to say upon hearing the verdict she replied, "Although I have been found guilty, with the exception of my intimacy with Mr. Brierley, I am not guilty of this crime."[46]

In 1892, three years after Florence Maybrick's conviction, Sydney Grundy's *A Fool's Paradise* opened at the Garrick Theatre. The critic H. Chance Newton claimed that "disguise it as he would, Grundy had dramatized the great Maybrick Mystery in every detail,"[47] but in actuality, with the exception of the arsenic flypaper, there is no trace of the original case in this play. The villainess, Beatrice, is poisoning her unsuspecting (and adoring) husband because her old lover, Ned (who happens to be her husband's best friend) has returned. Being a man of honor, Ned wants nothing to do with Beatrice, preferring to court her companion (who is actually her husband's sister from another marriage, though no one knows this). The family doctor/detective solves the case, and Beatrice is caught before her husband dies. In true melodramatic fashion, she swallows poison and expires before she can be arrested for her crime.

Grundy's play, if it can be said to be based upon the Maybrick trial at all, is a very shallow treatment of a case that caused considerable controversy. Though the twelve men of the jury were convinced of Florence's guilt, the women of England were far more sympathetic to her cause. Hundreds of women attended Florence Maybrick's trial, many standing vigil for days outside the packed courtroom. The overwhelming number of the silent female spectators caused considerable consternation in the British press. A Liverpool paper castigated these "creatures called ladies," believing they attended the trial only out of a prurient interest:

What filth they must have in their hearts! What greed of lustful curiosity! What smug hypocrisy in their offenseless faces! What a dunghill of dirt seething and stinking behind their modest eyes and placid brows! For the women there is no excuse! Nothing but a prurient thirst for beastliness can account for their being there at all! In a place that every true woman should shrink from and abhor as she would a gaol or a brothel![48]

What the gentleman from Liverpool did not report to his readers was the fact that these women were not there to gape at Florence Maybrick, they were there to support her. When Florence was convicted women cried out in fury, and almost half a million people, mostly women, signed petitions to the Home Office demanding a reprieve. Many wrote to the newspapers in protest, and a sampling of their letters indicates how bold women were daring to be in public:

> Of course the jurors decided for their sex. Doubtless each one was a husband and became bitter on a dishonoring wife. (*Daily Post*, 15 August 1889)

> Crime is crime irrespective of sex. But to "stone" a weak woman for the same crime a man is allowed to commit with impunity [adultery] is not by any means fair play. (*New York Herald, London edition*, 14 August 1889)[49]

Eventually the campaign to free Florence Maybrick gained many male supporters, and through the efforts of American newspaperwomen, thousands of outraged women in the United States joined their voices in protest against a legal system that continued to equate a woman's adultery with murder. As one woman writes, "If this sentence is carried out, immorality and murder will be synonymous terms."[50] The protests did have an effect; Florence Maybrick's death sentence was commuted to life in prison.

Justice Stephens, like Sydney Grundy in *A Fool's Paradise*, may have wished to mold Florence Maybrick into a two-dimensional Victorian villainess, but many Englishwomen and men fiercely protested that representation. Florence Maybrick, adulteress, may have been convicted of murder by the state, but there can be no doubt that she was acquitted by the jury of her peers.

chapter 3

a jury of her peers[1]

This is what women have to stand on squarely; not their ability to see the world the way men see it, but the importance and validity of their seeing it some other way.[2]

Some day, perhaps *mulier* and *foemina* alike will covet the recapture of that old status of obedience. Meanwhile, and in the flush of possessing more Woman's Rights than are easily digestible, you embark on your career as a business woman, a wife, a mother with responsibilities, you should *understand*, or you may come a cropper.[3]

IN 1927 a thirty-two-year-old Long Island housewife kissed her young daughter good night, then walked into the master bedroom and watched her lover bash her sleeping husband's head in with a sash weight. Stories of domestic murder appeared daily in the New York papers, but this one, the murder of Albert Snyder by his wife, Ruth Snyder, and her lover, Judd Gray, captured the nation's attention. For eight months the country was obsessed with the Snyder/Gray trial; over 180 reporters from across the nation were assigned to the case, and readers hung on every word they wrote. When the two lovers were finally convicted and sentenced to die in the electric chair there was, literally, dancing in the streets.[4] When Ruth first learned that her jury would be all men, she said, "I'm sorry. I believe that women would understand this case better than men."[5] Ruth Snyder's wish for a jury of her peers was denied, and the press, almost exclusively men, painted the all-too-familiar picture of an abnormal woman driven to murder by her uncontrollable sexual appetite. One journalist, however, had a radically different impression of the crime. Sophie Treadwell, an experienced reporter turned playwright, was a spectator in the courtroom,[6] and her expressionist drama *Machinal* is clearly a dramatic revisioning of the Snyder/Gray trial. In contrast to the press and prosecutors who represented Ruth as a deviant woman, an aberration far removed from the feminine ideal, Treadwell rejected the notion that femininity and criminal behavior are mutually exclusive and implied that any woman could find herself in Ruth Snyder's position. *Machinal* presents Treadwell's version of the Snyder case, a case in which a normal woman, "any woman," when confronted with depressingly ordinary circumstances, finds she has no other option but to murder her husband if she is to save her sense of self. In *Machinal* Treadwell posits that a woman's natural state is not matrimony and motherhood but that those roles are forced upon her by a patriarchal culture that relies on female submission and self-sacrifice.

Ruth Snyder provides an excellent case study for examining the representation of a murderess in early-twentieth-century America; her case resonates with all the social anxieties evoked by feminist emancipation. Ruth seemed to embody a dangerous New Woman not bound by any moral or social code. Depicted by the prosecutor and the press as a woman who posed a serious threat to the American way of life, Ruth was used as an example to those women who might take their new "freedom" too literally. The Snyder case, as staged in the courts and in the press, became the great morality play of the decade, and as Ann Jones points out in *Women Who Kill*, it was meant almost exclusively for the edification of women.[7]

In the press, the crime of Ruth Snyder and the emergence of the New Woman were related events; emancipation and criminality blurred in the public discourse surrounding the trial. Many reporters depicted the murder of Albert Snyder as symptomatic of a profound social crisis. As they saw it (and wrote it) murder was only the final act in a long, sordid history of family obligations betrayed and common decencies violated.[8] The New Woman no longer felt compelled to love, honor, or most importantly, obey, and Ruth Snyder represented the inevitable outcome of this dangerous development. W. L. George, in a book entitled *The Intelligence of Women* (1920), writes that

> The "New Woman," as we know her today is a very unpleasant product; armed with little knowledge, she tends to be dogmatic in her views and offensive in argument. She tends to hate men, and to look upon Feminism as a revenge; she adopts mannish ways, tends to shout, to contradict, to flout principles because they are principles; she also affects a contempt for marriage which is the natural result of her hatred for men.[9]

Like many Americans, men and women alike, George was appalled by what he perceived to be the corrosion of virtuous womanhood and its inevitable consequence—the total disintegration of order in the home. Numerous editorials warned that the American family was disintegrating: the birthrate was down, the divorce rate was skyrocketing, and marital fidelity seemed a thing of the past. Between 1867 and 1929 the divorce rate in the United States had increased twenty times over;[10] to make matters worse, one-third of the nation's couples were childless and the birthrate was falling steadily.[11] In the minds of many Americans the roots of this social malaise could be traced directly to the emancipation of women and the subsequent disintegration of traditional gender roles. In *Statistical Analysis of American Divorce* (1932) Alfred Cahen writes that "woman's freedom or the modern emancipation of the wife from dependence on the husband is asserted to be a leading cause of divorce by most judges."[12]

Medical discourse was also employed to undercut women's legislative emancipation. In *The Nervous Housewife* (1920) Dr. Abraham Myerson concludes that it was the neurotic wife, not the emancipated New Woman (who would marry her anyway?) that had caused the staggering increase in divorce. He reasons that a woman's neurosis caused her to make unreasonable demands on her husband's patience, which in turn poisoned the marriage relationship and led to the disintegration of the family. "Having become more individualized *they demand more definite individual treatment and rebel more at what they consider an infringement of their rights as human beings. . . .* This has brought about the divorce evil"[13] (emphasis mine). All responsibility for domestic trouble is attributed to women who, having become "individualized" (expecting to be treated equally under the law), refuse to abide by the traditional rules of coverture. Dr. Myerson states that the "divorce evil" was caused by 1) women rebelling against the drunkenness, unfaithfulness, neglect, and brutality "that a former generation of wives tolerated and even expected";[14] 2) wives no longer accepting the idea that women are property; and 3) "the ill-balanced demands of women to be treated as equals and also as irresponsible, petty, and indulged tyrants."[15] Dr. Myerson resolves that "men are unable to adjust themselves to the shattering of the romantic ideal, and the home disintegrates."[16]

At the base of Myerson's argument is a disturbing reading of "romantic." If it was part of the "romantic ideal" that women expect and tolerate abuse, agree to be the property of their husbands, and never make demands, one has to ask, ideal for whom? Dr. Myerson, laying out the history, symptoms, causes, and cures for neurotic wives, codifies anxiety over feminine emancipation into medical fact by declaring that women with a "non-domestic nature" or "independent experience" are prone to neurosis. He predicts that if these two qualities "happen to reside in the same woman, then the neurosis appears in full bloom."[17] By diagnosing a woman who did not enjoy being a wife and mother as mentally ill, doctors like Myerson reinforced traditional notions of femininity and subtly undercut the achievements and goals of the emancipated woman.

Social anxieties surrounding the flagrant sexuality, deviant psyche, and lawlessness of the New Woman came together in the body of Ruth Snyder. She was seen as the worst case scenario, the neurotic housewife who, unable to contain her sexuality in the confines of her marriage, had tried to get away with murder. The murder of Albert Snyder was read as a direct attack on the American home, and as the home went, so went the nation. Ruth must be convicted, not to avenge her husband but to restore balance to a world caught in the flux of gender confusion. The prosecutor made it very clear to the jury just how high the stakes were in this case. "Gentlemen, our whole great nation, all of our American institutions are built and founded upon the sanctity of the American home, and if in this case there should be a failure of adequate punishment, that foundation, that cornerstone of these American institutions will totter and fall."[18]

The Crime

On March 20, 1927, Albert Snyder was found murdered in his bed, beaten on the head with a blunt object, chloroformed, and strangled with a piece of picture wire. When the police arrived, his wife, Ruth, was discovered outside their daughter's room, bound and gagged. She told police she had been attacked by a tall Italian man and claimed to have fainted when he grabbed her. The small house had been ransacked, drawers were emptied, and Ruth's jewelry had been stolen. Police became suspicious when the "stolen" jewelry was found under Ruth's mattress, and when she neglected to ask after her husband, they felt sure she was involved in the murder. When Ruth was told her husband was dead, police said the tears she shed were "suspiciously few."[19]

After nearly twenty hours of questioning, Ruth Snyder confessed that, with her lover, Judd Gray, she had beaten her husband to death with a sash weight while her nine-year-old daughter slept in the next room. Later she would change her story to say that it was Gray who had masterminded the murder and that she had been unable to stop him. Ultimately, both Ruth and Gray were convicted of murder and executed at Sing Sing on January 12, 1928.

Albert Snyder's murder captured the attention of the public and created a media event of astonishing proportions. Over fifteen hundred people attended; for the first time in history, microphones and speakers were set up in a courtroom so that everyone could hear the testimony. One had to have a ticket to be admitted, and scalpers were ready, as always, to make a quick buck, selling tickets for fifty dollars apiece. Damon Runyon writes, "This remains the best show in town, if I may say so, as I shouldn't. Business couldn't be better. In fact, there is some talk of sending out a No. 2 company and 8,000,000 different blondes are being considered for the leading role. No one has yet been picked for Henry Judd Gray's part but that will be easy. Almost any citizen will do, with a little rehearsal."[20] Runyon's humorous rhetoric placed the criminal trial firmly in the realm of Broadway entertainment. He also implies that the star in this drama is clearly Ruth Snyder; Henry Judd Gray plays a supporting role at best.

The complex reality of Ruth and Albert Snyder's relationship was diluted and funneled into the easily digestible scenario of the stage melodrama. For those who could not get into the show, the newspapers, in column after column, recreated the trial in phenomenal detail: reprinting the testimony, reporting everything Snyder and Gray said or did, reviewing their performances on the stand, and keeping a running commentary on "audience" reaction. The *New York Times* ran an article on the trial almost every day from the morning of the murder to the night of the execution. By May 5, 1927 (according to the *Evening Post*), 1.5 million words about the Snyder story had been filed on press wires. A *New York Times* editorial lambasted the press for its obsession with the case. The writer imagined what the weekend recess of the court would do to reporters who could not get enough of this murder. "Imagine the anguish of the sentimental interpreter with all the emotion with which he is now compelled to bottle up for two days. The amount of suppressed philosophy, psychoanalysis which the adjournment of court will leave in so many stuffed bosoms is pathetic to contemplate. If any mysterious explosions are heard over Sunday, they will probably be due to the writers about the trial unable to contain themselves."[21]

The first day Ruth took the stand, the *New York Times* described the spectators in the courtroom as "a typical Broadway audience, sophisticated and cynical." In attendance were playwright Willard Mack, philosopher Will Durant, W. E. Woodward, Ben Hecht, Fannie Hurst, and Nora Bayes. Sophie Treadwell, though not officially covering the trial, was a spectator in the courtroom. Readers were as interested in the stars attending the trial as in the case, and the tabloids solicited celebrity opinions for their columns. The characters in the courtroom were easily recognizable: The Wife, The Lover, and The Cuckold. Journalists became stage managers, arranging the narrative, casting the characters, and manipulating audience response to this stock scenario.

What does not emerge in the press coverage of the Snyder/Gray trial is the abusive relationship Albert Snyder had with his wife and daughter. There was substantial evidence that Albert Snyder, who drank eight to ten highballs each evening, beat his wife and his child on several occasions. The couple quarreled often, and Ruth testified that her husband, who had recently bought a gun, had threatened to "blow her brains out."²² Ruth's attorney, trying to portray her as the model wife who stocked her cellar with homemade preserves, never brought up Albert Snyder's violence, but Judd Gray referred to the abusive relationship in his testimony:

> She said she could not live with him any longer. . . . I asked her if she really felt in her own mind that he would kill her. She said that he was liable to do anything. At that particular time she complained bitterly about his treatment towards their youngster. She said that he had slapped her on that particular day, and almost knocked her down. I asked her if that was usual. She said that he had slapped her many times and that that particular time she felt as though she could kill him.²³

What is remarkable about this statement is that Gray is testifying *against* Ruth. His acknowledgment that Albert slapped Ruth many times and had knocked her down that day provided two important pieces of information for the jury. First, it gave Ruth a motive for her violence, but more importantly it implied that Ruth was an undisciplined wife who had angered her husband. In 1927 there was no legal concept of a battered woman defense; if a woman was beaten by her husband, in moderation, that reflected badly on her, not on him.

The Defense

The opening statement, made by Judd Gray's attorney, set the tone for the entire trial. His defense argued that, on his own, Judd Gray was an upstanding, law abiding, red-blooded American male. His only flaw, and a tragic one, was a weakness of will that made him susceptible to the machinations of evil women like Ruth. Judd Gray was described as a good husband and father who, due to a weak-willed nature, had been lured into criminal behavior by a dominating woman. Even the prosecuting attorney called Gray "a decent, red-blooded, upstanding American citizen" in his summation.²⁴ Gray's attorney, attempting to shift the blame for the act onto Ruth, transfigured the rather ordinary Long Island housewife into an oversexed, machiavellian monster. His opening statement made it perfectly clear who he felt was the real villain in this story:

> [Gray] was dominated by a cold, heartless, calculating mastermind and master will. He was a helpless mendicant of a designing, deadly, conscienceless abnormal woman, a human serpent, a human fiend in the guise of a woman. He was in the web, in the abyss; he was dominated, he

was commanded, he was driven by this malicious character. He became inveigled and was drawn into this hopeless chasm, when reason was gone, when mind was gone, when manhood was gone and when his mind was absolutely weakened by lust and by passion and by abnormal relations.[25]

Both Gray and Ruth had a spouse and child, both had engaged in an adulterous affair, both had conspired to murder a man while he slept. Yet despite the symmetry of their crime, they were judged by entirely different standards. Ruth's most significant crime seems to be that she was a bad wife and mother. Reading the trial transcript one gets the impression that Ruth is being tried for adultery and not for murder; Albert's death is simply the regrettable outcome of Ruth's criminal and uncontrolled sexual passion.

Gray's attorney referred to Ruth as "an abnormal woman" over twenty times in his closing argument, clearly rooting this abnormality in her sexual activity outside of marriage. Addressing the jury he said, "She herself, in her own handwriting spoke of that burning blaze within her. She is abnormal gentlemen. She has always been abnormal."[26] Lawyers and press alike demonized and defeminized Ruth, calling her a "fiend wife," "woman of steel," "marble woman," "flaming Ruth," and "vampire." Ruth was distanced from other women whenever possible, and since "normal" women were faithful, nurturing wives and mothers, Ruth was clearly defective. Willard Mack writes, "If Ruth Snyder is a woman then, by God! you must find another name for my mother, wife or sister."[27]

In the early newspaper reports of the murder Ruth was described as the "beautiful wife" of the slain art editor; but as the trial progressed reporters changed their description of the widow. By the time she took the stand, according to the press, Ruth didn't even look like a woman anymore.[28] The once "attractive blonde" was suddenly "heavy and coarse" and was reported to have a "masculine jaw, rough skin, straight hair, and a wrinkled dress." The rhetoric of Lombrosian criminology, which cited masculine physiognomy as indicative of a criminal nature in women, was in full force. It was easier to accept that an abnormal, masculine woman was guilty than to live in a world where attractive blondes could kill their sleeping husbands.

Ruth's defense attorney countered the attack on Ruth's femininity by drawing the picture of a model homemaker, enthusiastically describing the homemade preserves Ruth stocked in the cellar and the hand-sewn curtains that decorated the Snyder home. But his most telling defense came in the summation, when he described the birth of Ruth's daughter, Lorraine:

> Do you mean to tell me that a woman in the throes of agony of childbirth, who gave this beautiful baby to the world and to Snyder after a severe

operation, which might have wrecked her health forever; do you mean to say that there lives that woman on earth that would have brought home that baby to perhaps see the spectacle of the mother sending that baby's father to eternity? *That woman don't live, and not one of you twelve men believe she does. And it stands out, that testimony, more eloquent than any words that can be uttered* by me or any other advocate pleading for a cause that he believes as just.[29] (Emphasis mine)

The strongest defense Ruth's attorney could offer was that she was a mother, and a mother would never be capable of a violent attack on her child's father. In the logic of the culture, Mother was the epitome of Woman, and Woman was incongruent with Criminal. Ruth's attorney declared that her willing acceptance of motherhood, despite the difficulty she had conceiving, was stronger proof than any other testimony that Ruth was incapable of murder. A mother who could kill? "That woman don't exist." Either she was a true woman and not guilty, or she was, as the prosecutor claimed, merely a fiend in the guise of a woman.

This either/or criminology is consistent with the either/or options being presented to women of the period. Either you are Wright's New Woman (dogmatic, revengeful, and mannish), or you are Jessup's Womanly Woman (coveting the old characteristic of obedience). Either you are content with marriage and motherhood or you are neurotic, "rebelling at what [you] consider an infringement of your rights as a human being."[30] Either you tolerate and expect abuse, as your mothers and grandmothers did before you, or you become, as Dr. Myerson so eloquently deduced, a mentally ill, "irresponsible, petty and indulged tyrant."

The Judgement

Despite her lawyer's efforts Ruth was found guilty, and on May 13, 1927, both she and Gray were sentenced to die in the electric chair. Though the jury did not acquit Gray, they did feel he was an honorable man led astray by a monstrous woman. After the verdict one juror told the *New York Times* reporter, "There was little doubt in any of our minds as to what the verdict would be. We all knew that Mrs. Snyder was lying. We all believed every word that Gray said."[31] Mildred Gilman, journalist and author of the novel *Sob Sister* (1931), felt that Ruth Snyder "would have escaped with a life sentence if she had played a different role with the press. She slipped into the 'iron woman' category instead of the 'sympathetic, misunderstood wife.'"[32]

As it was, Ruth had few supporters. Popular opinion was entirely behind the verdict, and thousands lined up to watch the prisoners being brought to the death house at Sing Sing. In *Ladies of the Press,* journalist Ishbel Ross describes the scene outside Sing Sing on the night Ruth Snyder was electrocuted:

> On the night that Ruth Snyder died, Miss McCarthy, who was then on the *Journal,* was one of the newspaper women who waited outside the prison while a huge crowd made shocking whoopee at the gates. It might have been a carnival instead of an execution. . . .There were children and Boy Scouts. Vendors sold hot dogs and popcorn. It was like a Roman holiday. . . . The most seasoned reporters were startled by the antics of this ghoulish crowd. Brick Terrett, came out after it was over. He had seen Ruth die in the chair. "Julia, for God's sake take a walk with me," he said to Miss McCarthy. "Talk to me about anything. My God, she looked so little." Another man who had come out with him from witnessing the same scene vomited on the spot.[33]

College boys and boy scouts partied in the streets while Ruth Snyder, the constructed embodiment of feminist emancipation, was about to "cook, and *sizzle,* AND FRY!"[34] in the electric chair. Those who knew Ruth only through the press' representation of her celebrated the execution of a monstrous aberration, while those who had been inside had seen a real woman die.

The day after Snyder and Gray were executed, columnist Nunally Johnson summed up the entertainment value of the courtroom drama that had captivated the nation: "It was a grand show. It never failed once. It had no surprises, no Theatre Guild stuff, no modernisms. It was the good old stuff done well and fiercely. It was grim and grand. It moved slowly and inevitably like Dreiser. And it came at last, last night, to the magnificent, the tremendous, the incomparable curtain that the audience was counting on. Everybody walked out with a satisfied feeling."[35]

Johnson could feel satisfied because the script for this trial followed nineteenth-century melodramatic convention, which as we saw in the case of Mary Edmondson, erases all ambiguity. In melodrama, Good is distinct from Evil, Justice always prevails, and the hierarchy is preserved. Johnson's comment indicates his preference for the predictable genre of melodrama and his attendant discomfort with modern dramatists who attempted to complicate issues of right and wrong.

During the trial Peggy Hopkins Joyce wrote the following:

> And so I say there is no excuse for Ruth Snyder. Maybe if I knew the woman intimately I could find something that would explain her kissing her lover and sash-weighting her husband to death almost simultaneously. But looking at her in court where she is on exhibition as a sort of blue-ribbon defendant

and where she is supposed to be trying to impress a jury with her innocence, I shudder. *How did she get that way?*[36] (Emphasis mine)

As Treadwell watched the trial unfold she must have asked herself the same question: "How did she [Ruth] get that way?" The American press answered Joyce's question by declaring that Ruth Snyder was an aberration, a product of women's unnatural emancipation and the inevitable neurosis that followed. That answer didn't satisfy Treadwell, and *Machinal* was her response.

Eight months after Ruth Snyder's execution, *Machinal*, directed by Arthur Hopkins and designed by Robert Edmund Jones, opened at the Plymouth Theatre in New York City, just a few miles from the prison where cheering crowds had gathered to see Ruth "fry" in the electric chair. In a last-minute attempt to save Ruth's life, her attorneys had asked that an alienist (psychiatrist) be brought in to testify on her behalf. Hoping to save their client, the lawyers wanted to examine Ruth's mind "in light of modern science." The governor denied the request. It is possible to look at *Machinal* as Treadwell's attempt to examine Ruth's mind in the light of modern drama, giving her, ironically, an appropriately theatrical life-after-death. One can read *Machinal* as the testimony, disallowed by the court of law, that Treadwell wished to introduce into the court of public opinion.

The prosecutor had attempted to construct a demon, a fiend woman whose violence was explained by her deviation from the feminine ideal. One journalist for the *New York Evening Post*, apparently not accepting this explanation, asked the following:

> How then does Mrs. Snyder differ from those other dissatisfied wives with heavily insured husbands? Or from the subtle women who meet men without their husbands' knowledge? We do not know the answers to these questions, and will perhaps never know them. The law does not try to find out; it deals only with events and with the superficial motives leading to them. So here is the real mystery in the Snyder case. It is the profound mystery of personality. The mystery of impulses.[37]

It is precisely the mystery "of personality and impulse" that Treadwell explores in *Machinal*, using an expressionistic style to enter freely the subconscious mind of her subject, to look beyond the "events and superficial motives" that were revealed in the courtroom, and question the court's assumption of cause and effect. *Machinal* asks if there might not be a more complex, psychological reality involved in the murder of Albert Snyder. In *Machinal* surface details differ, often substantially, from the Ruth Snyder story. This led most reviewers to write that the play was only loosely based on the Snyder case. But just as an expressionist painting reveals the inner life of its subject rather than the outer, so *Machinal* explores the subtext of the trial whose surface details were so well known to "the Broadway crowd."

Treadwell begins the play with what some have seen as a disclaimer of the connection to Ruth Snyder. "THE PLOT is the story of a woman who murders her husband—an ordinary young woman, any woman."[38] But rather than distancing the play from the real trial, this statement articulates the subliminal fear that made Ruth Snyder so threatening and so interesting in the first place. In an analysis of the case, written for law students in 1938, John Kobler explains the fascination Ruth Snyder had for the average citizen:

> Psychotic freaks who go in for fancy dismemberment and other baroque horrors may momentarily titillate the old gentleman in carpet slippers, but when *Mrs. Jones* next door laces her husband's chowder with weed killer that same old gentleman is jounced off his perch. The thing is too near home, too understandable. Subconsciously he identifies himself with poor Jones. He may even view his own consort in fresh perspective—and wonder a little.[39]

The prosecuting attorney proved that Ruth killed her husband to get out of an unhappy marriage, but how was the Snyder marriage different from thousands of other unhappy marriages? If the trial could not explain what made this particular unhappy wife kill her husband, then subliminally, all wives would become suspect. Ruth's very ordinariness was her danger.

In *Machinal* the Young Woman, like Ruth Snyder, is an office worker who marries her much older boss. She does not love him, but she welcomes the security that his money provides. In the second episode, entitled "At Home," the Young Woman confesses her doubts about her future husband to her Mother. She describes the feelings of revulsion she experiences whenever he touches her:

> YOUNG WOMAN: Tell me—Your skin oughtn't to curl—ought it—when he just comes near you—ought it? That's wrong ain't it? You don't get over that, do you—ever, do you or do you? How is it Ma—do you? (192)

Treadwell spends considerable time establishing the unhappiness of the Young Woman's marriage. This in contrast to the real trial, where the defense attorney, attempting to portray Ruth as a good wife, shied away from the unpleasant facts of this marriage, which seemed doomed from the start. Ruth Snyder had fallen ill on the day of her wedding and after the ceremony refused to leave with her husband, so on their wedding night,

Albert Snyder went home alone while Ruth stayed with her mother. Treadwell interprets that night in the third episode of *Machinal*, entitled "The Honeymoon." While happy couples dance below her, the Young Woman, repulsed by her husband on their wedding night, cowers by the bed, calling for her mother.

> YOUNG WOMAN: Ma Ma! I want my mother!
> HUSBAND: I thought you were glad to get away from her.
> YOUNG WOMAN: I want her now—I want somebody.
> HUSBAND: You got me haven't you?
> YOUNG WOMAN: Somebody—somebody—
> HUSBAND: There's nothing to cry about. There's nothing to cry about. (200)

Treadwell's Young Woman weeps on her wedding night, disgusted by the touch of her husband's hands on her legs. He pinches her and tells her dirty jokes, and when she recoils from his kiss he scolds, "You've got to learn to relax little girl—haven't you?" (198) Gray, in his testimony, described a conversation he had with Ruth at their second meeting. "She said she had never really known what sexual pleasures were with her husband. I sympathized with her, as I recall, that it was too bad, as I felt that was probably one of the greatest reasons for her unhappiness. She told me that when he came over into bed with her that to her *it was so disgusting and degrading that she felt like killing him*"[40] (emphasis mine). The experience of having your body used by a man you do not love was probably not one that the male jury could sympathize with or understand. Ruth's attorneys never used this line of reasoning in her defense, but in *Machinal* Treadwell makes the Young Woman's sexual degradation a central part of her testimony against the system that convicted Ruth Snyder.

Ruth cried only three times on the stand, a fact used against her by her detractors in the press—would not a real woman have wept? The first time Ruth cried was when she described her husband's anger that she had given birth to a girl and not a boy. Despite her obvious affection for her daughter, the experience of her birth was very traumatic both emotionally and physically, and Ruth developed painful abscesses of the breast soon after giving birth. In light of the Motherhood defense, offered by Ruth's attorney, Treadwell's scene of the childbirth is fascinating. In the fourth episode, entitled "Maternal," the Young Woman lies silent in a hospital bed, the sounds of riveting outside the window grating on her nerves. Treadwell portrays childbirth with all its psychic pain, and the jackhammers and drills in the background refuse to let us romanticize the event. The Young Woman will not breast-feed the baby, and when her husband brings her flowers she begins to gag. The doctor sighs, echoing Dr. Meyerson's diagnosis in *The Nervous Housewife*. "These modern neurotic women, eh. What are we going to do with 'em? Bring the baby!" (203)

The Young Woman is resentful and bitter, barely able to speak her revulsion at the thought of ushering another life, in particular another female life, into a world that is suffocating her. Birth is reduced to its most animalistic essence, and the Young Woman, utterly dehumanized, identifies herself with a dog giving birth in a pool of blood:

> YOUNG WOMAN: . . . Vixen crawled off under the bed—eight—there were eight—a woman crawled off under the bed—a woman has one—two three four—one two three four—one two three four—two plus two is four—two time two is four—two time four is eight Vixen had eight—one two three four five six seven eight—Puffie had eight—all drowned—drowned—drowned in blood—blood—oh God! God—God never had one—Mary had one—in a manger—in the lowly manger—God's on a high throne—far—too far—no matter. (205)

Unlike the defense attorney, Treadwell will not locate Ruth's defense in motherhood. Rather, the societal obligation to bear children is presented as a cruel imposition.

Painted by the press and prosecutor alike as the innocent and unsuspecting cuckold murdered in his sleep by a traitorous wife, trial testimony reveals that Albert Snyder was in fact an angry, violent man. A neighbor interviewed years after the murder recalled a day when he had broken Snyder's window with a fly ball. He said Snyder came at him with a "blazing temper, face distorted and purple," and beat him with "huge, powerful hands."[41] On another occasion Snyder, upset by a waiter's inattention, overturned a table and stormed out of a restaurant. In *Machinal* Treadwell does not portray a violent husband, but the Young Woman is fixated on her husband's hands, which are fat and repulsive to her.

Gray's testimony reveals Albert Snyder's abusive behavior. In light of this abuse, the sixth episode, entitled "Intimate," which is a scene where the Young Woman discovers love for the first time after years in an unhappy marriage, resonates with compassion rather than judgment. Treadwell shows the Young Woman, who has never experienced love or pleasure at the hands of her husband, in a moment of supreme happiness as sexual passion is finally awakened. She emphasizes the importance of this scene by returning to a naturalistic style of dialogue, asserting that this "illicit" love is more natural and necessary than the degrading sexual manipulation of the woman's marriage. At first the lover, Richard Roe, an adventurer who travels to exotic places, seems a far cry from Judd Gray, the corset salesman from Syracuse. But to Ruth Snyder, whose husband kept her close at home, Gray's life as a traveling salesman represented freedom and adventure. In the court testimony she says that accompanying Gray on a ten-day sales trip across New York State was the happiest time of her life. Looking not at the outward details but at the internal desires of an unhappy woman, Roe and his exotic travels can be seen as a romanticized version of Judd Gray the traveling salesman.

The public condemned Ruth for her sexual relationship with a man who was not her husband, and in their eyes she was a fallen woman. But Treadwell uses the affair and the awakening of sexual passion to bring the Young Woman, finally, into the fullness of her womanhood. The stage directions for this scene are telling: *"her dressing is a personification, an idealization of a woman clothing herself. All her gestures must be unconscious, innocent, relaxed, sure and full of natural grace"* (224). When Roe asks the Young Woman if she has ever felt on top of the world, she replies, "Yes, Today. I never knew anything like this way! I never knew that I could feel like this! So—so, purified! Don't laugh at me!" (225) When he kisses her, "her eyes shine with tears." Ruth's extramarital affair may have been the most damning evidence against her, but Treadwell defends Ruth's infidelity by reversing the court's assumption that a woman's most important duty is to fulfill her husband and by asserting that a woman has a more important duty, which is to fulfill herself. In a radical revisioning of gender roles Treadwell redefines "true womanhood" as self-fulfillment, not self-sacrifice.

The most dramatic difference between *Machinal* and the Snyder case comes in the actual trial scene. Treadwell makes the Young Woman alone responsible for the murder of her husband. Her lover, aside from giving her the idea (by telling her how he once killed a man by hitting him on the head with a bottle full of stones), had nothing to do with the husband's death. But again, Treadwell is not looking at the surface details of the trial but at its subtext. It was always Ruth Snyder's trial: she was the focus of the media, she was perceived as the mastermind behind the murder, she was responsible for corrupting the innocent Gray. Although Gray inflicted the fatal blows to Albert Snyder's head, it was Ruth Snyder who bore the blame for the act. In *Machinal* it is a letter from her lover (safely ensconced in Mexico) that convicts the Young Woman; without that testimony she may have gone free. By having the Young Woman's lover convict her, Treadwell portrayed the political reality of Ruth's trial. It was the testimony of Gray, her codefendant, that ultimately convicted Ruth. There were no witnesses to the murder, so the case was a matter of his word against hers. In his summation, Ruth's attorney said, "Now I am going to remark at the outset, in no uncertain terms, that you gentleman might now understand, that *this is a case of Henry Judd Gray and the people of the state of New York against Ruth Snyder, and nothing else.* She is sandwiched in between two prosecutors and you know it, and the district attorney need only sit idly by and watch the condemnation of this woman by this co-defendant."[42]

"I'm sorry," Ruth Snyder had said, "I believe women would understand this case better than men." *Machinal,* a woman's story told by another woman, played for the same "Broadway crowd" that had seen Ruth Snyder condemned to die. It should have been easy for that audience, who had witnessed Ruth Snyder's trial just eight months earlier, to see the Young Woman as a profound reinterpretation of the "fiendish woman" who had died in the electric chair. Though the play was a critical success, the reviewers' inability to look beyond the surface differences of plot prevented them from appreciating Treadwell's defense of Ruth Snyder and her questioning of the inherent male perspective in the trial. Brooks Atkinson of the *New York Times* writes, "In superficial details the story resembles the Snyder and Gray murder case. But Sophie Treadwell, who is Mrs. W. O. McGeehan in private life, has in no sense capitalized a sensational murder trial in her strangely moving, shadowy drama. Rather she has written a tragedy of submission."[43] It is telling that Atkinson, who felt the need to define Treadwell in terms of her marital status by assigning her husband's name as her true identity, could not see a tragedy of submission in Ruth Snyder's story.

Robert Littell, in his review for *Theatre Arts Monthly,* also fails to see any significant connection between Treadwell's drama and the Snyder case:

> Sophie Treadwell was one of the newspaper women who witnessed the trial of Ruth Snyder and Judd Gray. This brutal, inhuman murder, one of the ugliest on record, gave her the starting point for *Machinal,* but only the starting point. Having seen the two monsters, and the motives which led them to kill Snyder, she forgets their story and their characters and asks herself, How is it possible for a sensitive woman of deep feelings to be so oppressed by life and by her husband that she kills him?[44]

Littell categorically dismisses the idea that Ruth Snyder might have feelings or sensitivities, and disallows the possibility that she may have been oppressed by life or brutalized by her husband. The need to keep Ruth an aberration is strong for these reviewers. Ironically, Littell ends up being so sympathetic to Treadwell's Young Woman that he says, "I cannot help feeling that Miss Treadwell would have been artistically more successful if she had stopped short of the end."[45] No doubt Ruth would have preferred that as well.

In a case study that provides a tantalizing coda to the Ruth Snyder saga, Dr. Myerson presents a case in *Nervous Housewife* that sounds remarkably like Treadwell's Young Woman. Echoing *Machinal*'s expressionistic technique, Myerson uses the convention of substituting letters for names, and it is ironic that both use the letter *J* as a signifier for their subject:

> From the very first night J's world was shattered . . . Cave-man style outraged her every fiber, and the man was dumbfounded at her reaction . . . she found herself at odds with her husband's tastes and conduct in little things . . . the gusto of his eating annoyed her and took away her own appetite. When they went to a play together the coarse jokes and the plainly sensuous aroused his enthusiasm. He lacked subtlety and could not understand the "finer" things of life. She finally realized she no longer loved him. It is doubtful if she realized this before the birth of her first and only child. She lacked maternal feeling and rebelled with bitter rebellion against the distortion of her figure which came with pregnancy. The nursing ordered by the doctor and expected by all around her nearly drove her "wild" she said for she felt like a "a cow" a "female." Indeed she reacted bitterly against the femaleness that marriage forced upon her and hated the essential maleness of her husband.[46]

Myerson records that this woman tried to be a good housewife and to love her husband but everything he did irritated her and she felt trapped in a "luxurious cage." The family physician told Myerson on the side that it was "just a case of a damn fool woman with everybody too good to her."[47]

Dr. Myerson told the woman that her reaction to her husband was "abnormal and finicky," recommended separation, and concluded that her prognosis was "not good." What is fascinating about this case study is that the same symptoms Myerson attributes to neurosis—frigidity, tension, lack of maternal feeling, the sensation of being trapped, dizzy spells, and "bitter rebellion"—Treadwell attributes to the lack of options open to a young woman who feels trapped in a loveless, hurtful marriage. The men who condemned Ruth to death, like Myerson, decreed it abnormal for a woman to reject the primacy of her identity as wife and mother. Treadwell critiques their assumptions of normalcy, taking Ruth's failure as a wife and mother and turning the tables by showing how those roles in fact *failed her*. By extending the argument beyond the case of a single woman, constructing the Young Woman as any woman, Treadwell argues that all women, not just some freak of nature, can feel trapped in the machinations of gender expectations.

In *Machinal* Treadwell does not overturn the verdict, but she does critique the masculine bias of a legal system that judged Ruth Snyder as much for her deviance from the constructed ideal of feminine subservience and passivity as for her crime. Treadwell's use of expressionist technique highlights her assertion that in this case, the female defendant's perspective was radically different from that of her judges. The difference in their perspectives, she argues, significantly impacted the verdict.

In 1977, when Ruth Snyder was long forgotten, the Washington State Supreme Court ruled in the case of Yvonne Wanrow that the standard of the reasonable man was inappropriate in the case of a woman who killed her rapist. In this case the judge ruled that the woman was "entitled to have the jury consider her action in the light of her own perceptions of the situation, including those perceptions that were the product of our nation's long and unfortunate history of sex discrimination."[48] In *Machinal* Treadwell had anticipated the legal concept of the "reasonable woman" by over fifty years.

chapter 4

totaled women:
the battered wife defense

One of these days Alice, pow! Right in the kisser!
— Ralph Kramden, *The Honeymooners*

ON THE COVER of *Time* magazine, March 14, 1977, the headline "Fighting the Housewife Blues" is superimposed over a stack of dirty dishes and a half-empty baby bottle. Propped up in front of the mess is a copy of Marabel Morgan's book *Total Joy*, sequel to the "wildly popular" *The Total Woman*.[1] Morgan's Pepsodent smile on the cover seems to beckon the reader, promising that if we follow her advice, our lives too will be filled with joy. Like the writers of "conduct books," in the nineteenth century, Morgan insists that a woman can find happiness in her marriage only "by pampering and submitting to her husband," and she attributes this advice, like everything she writes, to God's wishes.[2] "It is only when a woman surrenders her life to her husband, reveres and worships him, and is willing to serve him, that she becomes really beautiful to him. She becomes a priceless jewel, the glory of femininity, his queen."[3]

Morgan decided to write *The Total Woman* when she realized she was nagging her husband, "insisting on my rights and demanding what I thought was due me."[4] Her marriage was on the rocks, so after reading the Bible and several self-help books, Morgan developed a system to "put sizzle back in her marriage."[5] Her plan includes strategies such as smiling when you feel down, brushing and flossing your teeth so that you will always be kissable, catering to "your man's special quirks,"[6] and wearing erotic costumes to welcome your husband home from work.[7] The authors of the *Time* article, eager to rationalize the success of Morgan's hyperfemininity in the midst of a feminist resurgence, do their best to recast Marabel as a feminist entrepreneur who is getting rich by selling advice to unhappy housewives;

they seem vaguely relieved when Marabel admits she's been too busy lately managing her business to dress up in erotic costumes and seduce her husband underneath the dining room table.

The 1970s, like the 1920s, were years of intense feminist energy and activism, as a national women's movement focused its forces on a campaign for the Equal Rights Amendment to the Constitution. But while feminists argued for equal pay and sexual freedom, an alternative discourse of hyperfemininity, couched in the language of religion and traditionalism, manifested itself in books like Morgan's *The Total Woman*. As it had in earlier periods of feminist growth, a backlash advocating the traditional role of wife and mother separated women into one of two categories: the unfeminine or the hyperfeminine. In the rhetoric of the backlash, women who agitated for equal rights were assigned Lombrosian traits of mannishness, ugliness, and anger. Feminism was deviant and the Total Woman would have none of it. Diametrically opposed constructions of femininity, with very little middle ground, clouded rational debate to the extent that anti-ERA campaigns succeeded by raising the specter of women in combat or, even worse, shared toilets. When the Illinois senate failed to ratify the Equal Rights Amendment, the state director of Eagle Forum, an antifeminist group, told a *Newsweek* reporter, "It's a tremendous victory for women of traditional moral values. Now I'm going home to get supper for my family."[8]

A week before the story on Marabel Morgan was published in *Time*, a Michigan housewife, after thirteen years of physical and sexual abuse, poured gasoline around her sleeping husband's bed and lit a match. Then she walked out of the house, got into her car, drove to the police station, and turned herself in. The woman was Francine Hughes, and though she never considered herself a feminist, her name became indelibly linked with the women's movement. Feminists rallied around Francine Hughes, raising money, garnering publicity, and using her trial to raise the consciousness of an American public for whom the phrase "domestic violence" meant campus riots or terrorist threats. Answering the insistent claim of people like Morgan, that a woman's place is in the home, feminists pointed to Francine Hughes to show that "home" was often the most dangerous place a woman could be. The *New York Times* reported that Francine's trial was a "murder trial that feminists hope will result in a landmark ruling on a woman's right to defend herself from domestic abuse."[9] At the time Francine Hughes was arrested, a survey of a California state prison found that of thirty women who had killed their mates, twenty-nine had been abused and twenty of them had killed their victims in the course of protecting themselves or their children from further abuse.[10]

In the public discourse surrounding the trial, there was a subtle (and sometimes not so subtle) sense that battered women were a creation of feminist rhetoric. One reporter noted that "The plight of battered wives has become a feminist rallying cry." Hearkening back to Dr. Meyerson's diagnosis of the neurotic housewife, the reporter added that "until recently, most women whose husbands beat them seemed to accept such abuse as some kind of conjugal responsibility."[11] There is an implication in this observation that feminists were stirring up the waters, swaying otherwise obedient women into resisting their "plight." The judge who arraigned Francine refused to grant bail. "After all," he said, "what kind of a woman would burn her husband?"[12] Francine's lawyer, public defender Aryon Greydanus, realized that this would be the trial's central question and that if his client were to be acquitted it was essential he show the jury that the kind of woman who kills her husband "might be *any* woman" trapped in an abusive marriage.[13]

This chapter examines the case of Francine Hughes, the only woman in this study who confessed to a murder and still was acquitted by a jury of her peers. The national interest in Hughes, first as a newsmaker and then as the subject of a television drama, *The Burning Bed*, makes her a perfect case study for evaluating the impact of dramatic representation on the legal and cultural constructions of criminality and for analyzing how those constructions intersect and redefine each other. Because at the time of this writing Francine is still alive she also presents us with the opportunity to compare the constructed identity to the actual woman.

Though certainly not a new phenomenon, the "battered woman" as a recently created legal category is currently being constructed and negotiated in the public and judicial psyche. Francine's case had been the first highly publicized case of wife abuse in the country, and the television movie, aired as part of National Domestic Violence Week, was the first major movie about domestic violence to be broadcast on national television. Casting Farrah Fawcett as Francine indelibly wedded the two women in the American psyche, and Francine Hughes, or at least the Francine Hughes created by Farrah Fawcett, became for many the prototype of the battered wife. Each layer of representation, from trial to book to movie, simplified the very complex life of Francine Hughes, reducing her to a screen on which to project a message. For feminists she embodied institutionalized violence against women, for the antifeminists she was the apocalypse. For Farrah Fawcett, Francine Hughes was the role of a lifetime.

Francine married Mickey Hughes in 1964 at the age of eighteen. Neither had a job, and so they moved in with Mickey's parents. Not long after the wedding Mickey began hitting Francine. When the beatings continued, and

Mickey's parents did nothing to intervene, Francine left and went home to her mother. It was the first of many times that Francine would run away. However, she did not stay away for long; her mother forced her to return to Mickey when she realized Francine was pregnant.[14]

Francine testified that over that next several years Mickey beat her regularly. She called the police many times, but the officers could arrest him only if they had actually seen the violent act, and by the time the police arrived Mickey was usually sitting calmly in the living room. When the police left the beatings would begin again. Mickey's few arrests were for assaulting a deputy, not for hitting Francine. In *The Burning Bed* biographer Faith McNulty describes a typical fight. After smashing Francine's head against a mirror and punching her in the stomach and in the face, Mickey stopped and threw her in a chair:

> "You know you're a no-good fuckin' bitch, don't you? Why don't you answer me? Answer me or I'll knock your teeth down your throat."
> I didn't say anything.
> "Fat-assed cunt! Why don't you say it?"
> I sat there crying and he hit me across the face. Then he asked me again. Finally I said, "Yeah."
> "Yeah what? What are you?"
> "Yes I am one."
> "A what? Say it!"
> "I'm a no-good fuckin' bitch."[15]

Francine went to see a counselor, who suggested that she take assertiveness classes. She didn't go. "How do you assert yourself with a maniac?" she asked.[16] Mickey's parents refused to acknowledge the abuse, and Francine's mother, a battered wife herself, insisted that a woman belonged with her husband. Mickey was unemployed and drinking heavily; Francine, pregnant again, with no money and no family support, could not feed her children. When she applied for welfare she found that only the head of the family could request state assistance, and Mickey had refused to ask for help. One welfare official noticed her black eyes and suggested she file for divorce; when he gave her the papers she was amazed at how easy it was to get one. All she had to do, he said, was fill out the form and give the clerk seven dollars for the filing fee. "If I had seven dollars I wouldn't be here," she told him. In one of the few acts of kindness shown toward Francine, the welfare official gave her the seven dollars from his own pocket.[17]

Though she was several months pregnant, Francine divorced Mickey and moved into her own apartment. When her fourth child was born, Mickey came to see the baby. He said he had stopped drinking and wanted another chance. They argued when she said he could not come back, and Mickey left in a rage. Speeding through a red light, Mickey experienced a near fatal crash that kept him in the hospital for the next two months. Pressured by his family, and feeling tremendous guilt about the accident, Francine agreed to help nurse Mickey when he went home. She rented the house next door to Mickey's parents, telling herself it was just until he was well.[18] Before long Mickey was back in her house and the violence escalated; on several occasions Francine was taken to the hospital. Mickey was living off of her welfare check, often drinking up the money she needed for food. With four children and no money Francine felt trapped. She testified that every day she tried to plan her escape but Mickey had convinced her that he would find her wherever she went. In *The Burning Bed* Faith McNulty records the scare tactics Mickey used to intimidate Francine into staying: "Don't think you can leave me, you bitch! Not ever! You ain't ever gonna get rid of me! I'll find you wherever you go and when I do it won't be pretty. I'll kill you inch by inch. I'll kill your fucking ass!"[19]

Trying to gain some economic independence, Francine applied for an education grant and was accepted in a secretarial college. Mickey let her go for a while, but on the day of the murder he ripped up her books and made her burn them in the trash barrel outside their house. Then he sent the children upstairs and beat Francine for two hours. After the beating Mickey wanted sex. Francine testified that if she did not give in he would only beat her again, so she complied; when Mickey passed out on the bed, she fed the children and waited for her youngest child to come home from a friend's house. She had decided to pack up the children and just drive—she didn't know where. In her testimony Francine described her thought process before the murder:

> During that time I was thinking about all the things that had happened to me . . . my whole life . . . all the things he had done to me . . . all the times he had hurt me . . . how he had hurt the kids. I decided the only thing for me to do was to just get in the car and drive. . . . Just go. And not let anyone know where I was at. Just leave everything and never, never turn back. The kids said, "Let's not come back this time, Mommy." I remember thinking that we wouldn't because there wouldn't be anything.[20]

The prosecution based its premeditated murder charge on the fact that Francine sat with three of her four children for two hours before setting the fire. She explained that she was waiting for her fourth child to come home from a friend's house. Finally, when the child didn't come home after several hours, Francine told the children to get in the car, got the gasoline, poured it around Mickey's bed, and set him on fire. She immediately turned herself in.

The jury of ten women and two men acquitted Francine of the first-degree murder charge in just under seven hours of deliberation. The victim of thirteen years of physical and sexual abuse, Francine had committed an act that even ten years earlier would have sent any woman to prison if not the gas chamber, but the jury excused her violent act in what seemed to be a startling reversal of judicial precedent. However, Francine was not acquitted on the plea of self-defense; she was found not guilty by reason of temporary insanity.

As Ann Jones points out in *Women Who Kill*, insanity is the stock defense for women who murder their intimates. Women who kill their husbands have made the ultimate transgression against conventional gender expectations. To preserve the normalcy of those expectations, women who deviate from them have historically been constructed as irrational, insane, or sexually uncontrollable. The final verdict on Francine Hughes did not radically alter traditional explanations of female criminality. By judging Francine insane at the time of the murder jurors were walking a legal tightrope, trying to reconcile "private" acts of domestic violence with the public realm of law.

To many who had heard Francine's nightmarish story the verdict seemed just. Others felt she should never have been tried in the first place. But to some observers, Francine Hughes's acquittal set a dangerous precedent. In 1977 there were several highly publicized cases in which women were acquitted of murder charges on the basis of the sexual and physical abuse they had suffered at the hands of the victim.[21] A *Newsweek* reporter worried that the increased awareness of the pervasive physical abuse of women could have dangerous consequences. "However useful that may be to the feminist cause, the legal implications are worrisome . . . by broadening the principles [of justifiable homicide] for battered wives, courts may suggest the opposite—and if it is left to run its course, such a trend smacks uncomfortably of frontier justice."[22] The idea that a woman could be victim and murderess simultaneously, destabilized the law's central separation of guilt and innocence. Furthermore, it challenged deeply held notions of gender and power within the family. A sheriff in one case asked a *Time* reporter, "I wonder if these people know what they are doing. If they get their way, there's going to be a lot of killings."[23] Mickey Hughes's brother had only one comment on the verdict: "It's open season on husbands."[24]

To Build a Better Murderess

Two years after her acquittal Francine's story was published in a biography by Faith McNulty entitled *The Burning Bed: The True Story of an Abused Wife*. McNulty, a reporter for *New York Magazine*, had access to the trial transcripts and was able to interview many of the people connected with the case. She also had access to Francine's autobiography, written while Francine was in prison awaiting trial. McNulty spent many hours interviewing Francine, and in her preface notes that both she and Francine were very concerned that everything they wrote needed to be true, nothing invented or added for effect; still, McNulty acknowledges that there is a powerful absence in the book. "No one can speak for the man who was her partner in tragedy."[25] McNulty reconstructs the life of Francine and Mickey Hughes in graphic detail, and much of the text is written in the first person, from Francine's point of view. McNulty's role as narrator and constructor of the narrative is obscured by the book's confessional format.

Seven years after Francine's acquittal McNulty's book was made into a television drama, *The Burning Bed*. By this point Francine's character had already been presented to the public through several levels of representation: the courtroom arguments, the press response, the biography, and now the television movie. The dramatic interpretation, four times removed from the actual event, reached the largest portion of the population primarily because of the identity of the actress who was cast as Francine Hughes: Farrah Fawcett. The casting of Fawcett, one of the country's most popular "sex symbols,"[26] insured that millions of people across the country would "see" Francine Hughes's story.

Angelic Victim

From the start *The Burning Bed* is Farrah Fawcett's movie; her name fills the screen well before the title or any other physical image can establish a mood. The next sequence of images shows the gasoline being poured, a match being lit, and then Farrah walking out of the house toward three children in a car as the house bursts into flame. The movie starts with the inexplicable crime: Whom had she killed? Why did she do it? What kind of a woman could do a thing like that? The audience, like a jury first presented with a case, knows nothing. The film is told in flashbacks as Francine is interviewed by her lawyer; she is ostensibly the filter through which the story is told. But of course the camera, the director's eye, is the real filter, and that eye rarely strays from the face and body of Farrah Fawcett.

All of the prebroadcast publicity focused on the former angel of *Charlie's Angels*, the cover girl actress who epitomized American beauty and feminine charm. At thirty-seven, Farrah was the same age as Francine Hughes, but there the similarities ended. In an interview with *People* magazine she acknowledged that before *The Burning Bed* she "had never thought about wife abuse." She had done some research, attending battered women's shelters, and said she found it very hard to relate to the women there. In an interview with *Redbook* magazine she said, "When I first started doing the research I noticed that a lot of these women were overweight. They didn't seem to care about themselves. My first reaction—and I felt bad for feeling this way—was: 'Why don't you lose some weight? Why don't you *do* something?' I didn't have much sympathy for them."[27] The women's physical appearance affected her ability to empathize with their situations, and studies have shown that many jurors have the same reaction to women whose appearance falls short of current cultural notions of beauty.[28] Farrah's own physical appearance was considered an obstacle to her believability in the role; her makeup artist told the *New York Times*, "The first order of business was to tarnish her physical beauty . . . to disfigure her face is difficult for me. It's like putting your foot through a Rembrandt."[29]

Even without her usual glamorous look, Farrah could not shake the public's image of her as a cover girl. The *Time* reviewer, calling *The Burning Bed* "the best TV movie of the year," praised Fawcett's performance but could not separate her from her public persona as a national sex symbol. "Her cover girl face disfigured with cuts and bruises, the former *Charlie's Angel* movingly conveys both the helplessness and the courage of a woman trapped in a nightmare."[30] Another reviewer wrote, "It's downright painful to see one of our national sex symbols struggle as a victim of her sex. Sad-eyed and disheveled, Fawcett's portrayal of a woman trapped by her husband's cycles of beatings and remorse is a far cry from being a *Charlie's Angel*."[31]

The movie follows McNulty's book, simplifying some situations and condensing several others. The numerous times that Francine moved are reduced to one successful escape just before Mickey's accident. The language, in order to be broadcast on television, is toned down considerably, resulting in a much less verbally abusive Mickey. The director insisted that the fight scenes be staged as realistically as possible, and several reviewers claimed that the violence in the movie went well beyond the level necessary to tell the story. Despite these reviewers' complaints, the filmed violence is relatively mild in comparison to Francine's testimony. The first fights are heard and not seen, as the camera focuses on the reactions of those around the couple. People look concerned then go back to their business, children close their eyes, a neighbor closes his window to shut out the sound of Francine's screams. As the film progresses the violence itself becomes the focus, and the final fight is graphically filmed, blood, sweat, tears and all.

Though the film remains relatively true to McNulty's book there is one crucial difference that hearkens to the historical conflation of adultery and murder, and evokes the cases of Alice Arden, Ruth Snyder, and countless other women who were tried as much for their sexual desire as for their violent actions. Francine Hughes testified that after her divorce she had a brief affair with a security guard at the business college she attended in Lansing. They slept together once, and when Francine realized he was a married man she ended the relationship. While she was in prison, the man corresponded with her, promising that when she was released he would be waiting for her. She wrote him schoolgirl love letters, which fell into the hands of the prosecution after the man committed suicide. Despite the fact that she was legally divorced from her husband, the brief relationship was presented by the press and by the prosecution as an adulterous affair. They understood that adultery was the perfect motive for murder and would discredit Francine as an "innocent victim." The headline of the *State Journal* trumpeted the startling news and quickly shifted Francine's actions from self-defense to adulterous betrayal. "MRS. HUGHES ACCUSED OF ILLICIT AFFAIR — Francine Hughes was having an intimate relationship with an unidentified man, and that was the key to her actions last March when she set a fire that killed her ex-husband, the prosecution concluded yesterday."[32] McNulty goes to great lengths to describe the relationship, Francine's response to it, and the defense's strategy for minimizing its effect on the jury. As McNulty represents it, Francine was vulnerable to a womanizing man, and given her miserable relationship with Mickey, it was only natural that she would respond to another man's attention and kindness. Apparently the jury agreed. The more problematic question, which no one seemed to ask, was why should an unmarried woman's sexual encounter (with a man who represented himself as unmarried) be construed as adultery?

Though the affair was prominent in both the trial and the book, the film makes no mention of it. The significance of this omission must be seen in the overall context of the film's reception. The filmmakers seemed to understand that their audience might have difficulty identifying with Francine in spite of Fawcett's tremendous popularity. In Farrah's body Francine was the perfect victim: she was a good mother and wanted nothing more than to be a good wife; she was an angel, the Total Woman of American fantasy. The final omission of adultery simply insures that through the body of Farrah Fawcett, the battered wife who kills her husband has been packaged for easy consumption.

In several interviews, Fawcett reinforced the gender role stereotypes that the movie exploits. She told an interviewer from *People* magazine, "I don't consider myself a feminist," and when asked why husbands beat their wives she played to antifeminist rhetoric by associating the onset of abuse with the women's movement. "I think it's largely due to the confusion of roles today. My parents had a traditional, loving relationship where he was big and strong and the breadwinner, and she took care of the home. Today men come home from a stressful day at work to find wives who demand equal say because they work too. Men traditionally have dominated and their masculinity is threatened."[33]

Even with the hyperfeminization of Francine's character, the filmmakers take no chances. In the final courtroom scene the camera focuses only on the lawyers and the witnesses. There is only one reaction shot, a remarkably slow pan from Francine to her lawyer, past the jury, the spectators, and finally out the door to her children, who are waiting in the hallway. One by one the faces in the crowd register shock, disbelief, and disgust as Francine's voice describes Mickey's abuse. It is the only time in the film when we are able to see anyone listening to, and caring about, her experience. They are outraged and by extension so are we.

But the abuse Francine is describing in the voice-over did not happen to her and it did not happen to her children: it happened to their dog. While Lady was in labor, Mickey refused to let her inside, and when the temperature dropped below freezing, the dog and her puppies froze to death. McNulty described this moment in the courtroom. "As Francine described Lady's death a shock wave of emotion swept the courtroom. The simplicity of the event—a helpless animal, a female, left outside to freeze while struggling to give birth—held no ambiguity, no shadings of motive; it left no room for doubt. The impact of the story was as strong as anything Francine had told so far."[34] The implication in this passage and in the cinematic treatment of this moment is clear and quite disturbing: descriptions of the attacks on Francine—who on many occasions had been locked outside to freeze, or beaten unconscious, or raped—these attacks were ambiguous, with "shadings of motives and room for doubt." Even in a case involving abuse so brutal as that inflicted by Mickey Hughes upon his wife, the defense was aware that its emotional trump card was the violent treatment of the dog and not the woman. In *Justifiable Homicide: Battered Women, Self-Defense and the Law*, Cynthia Gillespie writes, "We, as a nation, suffer from a painful ambivalence about violence against women. We simultaneously deplore it and excuse it. Far too often, instead of blaming the perpetrator of the violence, we go to great lengths to find ways to blame the victim."[35] Had the prosecution been able to find any excuse for "blaming"

Mickey's violence on Francine's behavior, they would have made it a centerpiece of their case. They tried, unsuccessfully, to frame the crime as the act of an adulterous wife eager get rid of an inconvenient husband, and had Francine not been legally divorced at the time of the affair, the prosecution's tactic might have succeeded. Likewise, the movie's producers, understanding the public's ambiguous response to domestic violence, knew they risked losing audience sympathy for Francine if she was depicted as anything less than perfect. Through Fawcett, Francine became an angelic victim, but there were still those who saw the film as part of a plot to exonerate a husband killer. In one review the critic is unabashedly opposed to the movie's tactics and the trial's outcome. *"The Burning Bed* is the most violent TV movie I have ever witnessed. It's obvious why the movie makers feel they must give viewers graphic illustrations of the brutality she underwent, in order to justify her murdering her husband, then beating the rap by pleading temporary insanity."[36] This reviewer also has trouble seeing Mickey, his family, or the social services that did not intervene as responsible for the tragedy. He concludes his review still wondering *"who* is the villain? I can't quite buy Hughes as the saintly heroine of feminist mythology."[37] Several reviewers seemed to feel that Mickey's violence was inexplicable and therefore tried to locate the blame somewhere else. One reviewer concluded that Mickey "just can't help it. He's not all bad, he's just an empty product of the American Dream that somehow never took root in the bleak Michigan landscape."[38]

The *Newsday* reviewer failed to see why the filmmakers had made the movie in the first place. He wanted Mickey's violence to be transcendent, to lead to a catharsis that would leave the audience purged of their social anxiety:

> The movie is totally horrifying. It's hard to imagine anyone watching this as entertainment. . . . What is the social usefulness and value of this well-meaning movie? . . . They are making a video record of the torture and degradation of this victim of society or whatever. . . . What does all this mean? What is transcendent about this experience? That's where art lies. There is no catharsis. That's why the authors will not be remembered like Strindberg or Ibsen in exploring the dark side of humanity.[39]

He concludes, "The point to a drama like this has to be how to get help, how to break the cycle. Otherwise what are they doing—teaching ignorance?"[40] In his final question he betrays his own inability to listen to a battered woman's story. Most of the movie is devoted to Francine's unsuccessful attempts to get help from her family, her neighbors, the police, and social service workers. This reviewer, like many who judge battered women who kill their abusers, read failure of response as a failure to seek help, and locate the blame for a woman's injuries on her "choice" not to leave.

Gender Stereotypes and the "Battered Woman Defense"

Battered women charged with killing their abusers present a dilemma to the criminal justice system. Myths and stereotypes about women and battered women play a prominent role in the courtroom presentation of both defense and prosecution cases. While the prosecution may attempt to discredit the defendant for not living up to the standard of a 'good woman', the defense counters with an equally distorted portrayal of the defendant as ultra-feminine: the passive helpless victim.[41]

There is actually no such thing as the "battered woman's defense." When defense attorneys argue that their client suffers from Battered Woman Syndrome they are in fact using expert testimony in support of a traditional self-defense plea. The Battered Woman Syndrome, which bears a strong resemblance to Post-traumatic Stress Disorder and is manifested in a variety of anxiety-related symptoms, was first introduced in a 1980 murder trial, where it was used to help the jury understand the life of a battered woman — to experience the prism through which she sees life and to judge her actions accordingly. Self-defense has always been an acceptable plea, but the judicial concept is predicated on the experience of two men in combat. In *Justifiable Homicide*, Cynthia Gillespie identifies the disadvantage women have when using this defense: "First, the law itself, which over many centuries has come to embody masculine assumptions about the circumstances that entitle a person to act in self-defense; and second, our society's ambivalent and biased attitudes about women and its acceptance of violence against them."[42]

Self-defense is defined as 1) using a justifiable and reasonable amount of force against an adversary, 2) believing that one is in immediate danger of unlawful bodily harm, and 3) using such force as is necessary to avoid this harm. The defendant must reasonably perceive imminent bodily harm; the perception may turn out to have been wrong but this does not nullify the defense.

These criteria may not apply in the case of a battered woman who kills her abuser. When two men of equal strength fight in a bar and one is killed, the law recognizes the principle of self-defense. A woman killing her sleeping husband in anticipation of abuse yet to come is clearly not self-defense as it has been traditionally defined. Is it, however, a reasonable action that a reasonable woman in the same circumstances might take? The key to defending the battered woman is establishing the reasonableness of her perceptions and subsequent actions.

Our legal code has evolved through a male tradition of jurisprudence, a tradition in which the "reasonable man" sets the decisive standard. How then to evaluate the reasonableness of a woman's act of self-defense?[43] The construction of the legal category "battered woman" appeared to be the answer to this judicial dilemma. If an abused woman can be identified and objectively diagnosed as having particular psychological traits, she can be given official sanction and factored into a stable legal discourse.

Ironically, while attempting to place the woman's perspective in the forefront of the judicial process, the use of the Battered Woman Syndrome in murder trials has ended up reinforcing traditional constructions of femininity. A 1984 New Jersey Supreme Court decision listed the following traits as typically exhibited by battered women: low self-esteem, traditional beliefs about the home, the family, the female sex role; tremendous feelings of guilt that their marriages are failing; and the tendency to accept responsibility for the batterer's actions. Though this list of traits accepted in court as typical of battered women allowed some women to benefit, those women who did not possess these traits, who did not appear helpless or espouse "traditional values," were looked on skeptically when they attempted to utilize the Battered Woman Syndrome in their defense. If a woman displayed anger, fought back, was unfaithful or in any other way "unfeminine," she found herself excluded from the constructed category of "battered woman":

> Legal and popular discourses separate "true" woman victims of domestic violence from the not really battered, undeserving viragos. The deserving victims are the upper middle class man's ideal bride, a Frankenstein creation of Mary Poppins, Mrs. Beeton and Barbie, "good mothers," "good wives," "good housekeepers," "good" heterosexual servicers who try, against all odds, to make a go of the marriage. Viragos generally fight back and are thus not really battered.[44]

As they had for centuries prosecutors continued to represent female defendants as bad mothers, promiscuous, or unfeminine in order to discredit them in front of the jury. Ironically, the Battered Woman Syndrome came to affirm the hierarchical understanding of gender that feminism had been "determined to dismantle."[45] While the 1977 case of Yvonne Wanrow, the Washington woman who killed her rapist, led to the creation of a "reasonable woman" standard, the question still remained, reasonable to whom? Any potential for a radically different feminist jurisprudence was constrained by the antiquated notions of acceptable feminine behavior that attached themselves to the concept of "reasonableness." The list of "unreasonable" women could include women who were angry or violent, women who were promiscuous or had had abortions, women who used drugs or committed other crimes such as prostitution or theft. If as one legal scholar noted, "any nontraditional female characteristic"[46] could disqualify a defendant from being considered a "good battered woman," then the power of those traditional feminine characteristics was just as strong as it had ever been. The accused woman was once again in the position of being categorized as either a monster or an angel, and neither construction of her character could represent the complexity of her life.

Francine Hughes Revisited

> The movie treats her acquittal with atrocious simple-mindedness, freeze framing on a smiling Francine being embraced by her children in the courtroom—i.e. sending the traditional TV signal that everything has been resolved, when nothing has or ever can be.[47]

Just before the broadcast of *The Burning Bed*, which aired seven years after Hughes's trial, *People* magazine ran a story on Francine Hughes.[48] On one page was a publicity shot of Farrah Fawcett in a prison uniform, blonde, angelic, and frail. On the facing page the real Francine Hughes, now thirty-seven and living with her children in a small tract house in Michigan, looks out from behind her window, "her cold eyes betraying a deep-seated distrust of strangers."[49] To one whose only exposure to Francine Hughes was Fawcett's portrayal in the television movie, her appearance is startling. She is a heavy-set brunette with small eyes and a double chin, lips compressed into a tight, thin line, and shoulders held stiffly against her neck; there is absolutely no physical resemblance between Francine and the actress who came to represent her in the pubic eye. It is the only in-depth interview that Francine ever granted, and though she is guarded she soon reveals that the differences between the real and fictional Francine Hughes are more than skin deep. The interviewer writes, "For Farrah, the TV docudrama provides the most challenging role of her life. For Francine, now 37, it tells only half the story."[50]

After her acquittal Francine worked as a secretary and then as a forklift operator at a factory. She told the interviewer that at that point in her life, she was out of control. "I was partying almost every night trying to escape from something. I drank a lot and was taking speed. It was like I was trying to self-destruct."[51] After being laid off from the factory she met and married Robert Wilson, a man on parole who had just completed ten years of a thirty-year sentence for armed robbery. There were tremendous fights between the children and their stepfather, and allegations of physical and sexual abuse eventually separated the family. Francine thinks that the accusations are probably true, but she still sees her husband on a regular basis.

Nine months in prison had created a deep rift between Francine and her children, and she admitted that "It was really hard for me to get close to them again."[52] Her oldest daughter, Christy, at age fifteen was smoking pot and "running around." Her son Jimmy sat around the house all day in his bathrobe, smoking cigarettes and drinking coffee. He "often knocked Dana down or smacked Nicole," and Wilson says he tried to "control [Jimmy] with fear."[53] Though the children accuse their stepfather of abuse, Wilson claims that Francine also hits the children. "Francine had to beat the tar out of Nicole a few weeks ago because she was misbehaving, and she blacked both Christy's eyes when she found her alone with her boyfriend."[54] The reporter noted that at the time of the interview, "Christy was still sporting slight bruises under her eyes. The fading shiners seemed frighteningly symbolic of other family wounds—wounds grown deeper and darker and more terrible with each passing year."[55]

It is of course mere speculation to wonder how the jury might have decided had they been able to see into the future. Would they have acquitted a woman who took drugs, married an ex-con, and hit her children? As the cases against battered women who kill their abusers are judged today, Francine may well have been found guilty of murder, her perfect victim status negated by her unfeminine, unmotherly behavior. Was the abuse she suffered any less real, or would the jury weigh Mickey's violence against Francine's transgressions and decide they balanced each other out? Under the current interpretation of the Battered Woman Syndrome, that is precisely what is happening today to defendants who are not "reasonable" women in the conservative eyes of the law.

Though wife beating is deeply rooted in the religious, legal, and cultural heritage of Anglo-American societies, a woman's violence against her husband has always been severely punished.[56] Though the laws may have changed, assumptions about a man's right to control his wife by force are deeply ingrained in our culture.[57] The year Francine Hughes was charged with first-degree murder, an Indiana prosecutor refused to prosecute for murder a man who had beaten and kicked his ex-wife in the presence of witnesses and then raped her as she lay dying. Filing for manslaughter instead, the prosecutor explained, "He didn't mean to kill her. He just meant to give her a good thumping."[58] In the same year, the International Association of Chiefs of Police training bulletin (written in 1968 but still in use in 1977) cautioned police who respond to domestic disturbance calls not to complicate the situation: "The officer should never create a police problem where there is *only a family problem existing*"[59] (emphasis mine).

Domestic violence has for centuries gone unchallenged behind the inviolable walls of the home; in the past decade spousal abuse has slowly come to light in large part due to the medium of television. One researcher in the field stressed the importance of mass media in bringing the realities of domestic abuse to the public attention. "After all," he wrote, "people do not respond to reality but to representations of that reality, making the role of the media in disseminating ideas and facts frequently crucial in influencing public opinions."[60]

Legal scholar Julie Blackman notes that the research literature of the 1970s and 1980s "created a rather singular image of the battered woman," and this image functioned as a standard against which other battered women were judged.[61] Numerous psychological studies have confirmed that jurors' preconceptions influence their perception of a defendant's guilt or innocence. In 1995 Daniel Yarmey conducted a study entitled "Facial Stereotypes of Battered Women and Battered Women Who Kill." He found strong evidence of the influence of television in developing a schema for facial types—lay persons were strongly influenced by television portrayals of criminals. "These results suggest that stereotypical perceptual images and myths about abused women continue to persist, in spite of all the writings and academic research on violence against women."[62] Studies like Yarmey's confirm that cultural representations of crime and gender matter a great deal in the formation of jurors' preconceptions. Due to the massive exposure received by *The Burning Bed*, Farrah Fawcett, in the role of Francine Hughes, participated in and became central to the creation of "the battered woman" standard, a standard that continues to affect the trials of battered women who kill their abusers today.

Aryan Greydanus's defense strategy was to make the jury see Francine Hughes's life through *her* eyes. Though television and film are uniquely suited to attempting a mode of personal narrative in which the camera's eye stands in for the eye of the woman who is experiencing the violence, it is rarely utilized in this way. *The Burning Bed* is a case in point. Rather than looking through Francine's eyes, it looks at her, and there is a tremendous difference between looking at Farrah Fawcett and seeing the world as Francine Hughes saw it. The detached observation of the camera reduces the characters, in particular Francine, to the conventional characterization of melodramatic notions of good and evil. The danger of objectifying good and bad as mutually exclusive categories has become apparent in a judicial system that now attempts to separate "deserving" victims of abuse from "undeserving" ones and punishes their resistance accordingly.

chapter 5

medea returns

> People are projecting their own fears onto me. Apparently hiring [a nanny] makes me, for many Americans, a dangerous character.[1]

TEN YEARS AFTER Farrah Fawcett had gotten the undivided attention of the television viewing audience with her performance as Francine Hughes, another woman was capturing television audiences in a real-life drama in Union County, North Carolina. On October 25, 1994, a twenty-three-year-old woman named Susan Smith reported her children missing. She told the sheriff that her car had been highjacked by an African American man, who drove off with her two young sons still strapped in their car seats. Local media zeroed in on the story, and composite pictures of the suspect, a black man in his thirties, were broadcast on every station. The local media were soon joined by national media, and the nation watched as Susan Smith pleaded with the kidnapper to return her children to her on the morning news programs of all three major networks.

After nine days of investigation into the kidnapping and after hours of television coverage of the search for the two boys, an astonishing revelation was made. Susan Smith had confessed. There had been no hijacking, no African American kidnapper; her televised pleas were all lies. She had killed her children by strapping them into their car seats and then letting her car roll into J. D. Long Lake. After confessing to the murder of Alex and Michael Smith, she begged the sheriff to give her his gun so that she could kill herself.

The television nation was horrified. News anchor Heather Hopes reported that the people of Union County were ready to "lynch Susan Smith," and the response was not limited to North Carolina. A national *Newsweek* poll revealed that 63 percent of those surveyed thought Smith should be executed, and images of the Salem witchcraft trials were evoked as crowds outside the courtroom chanted, "Burn her! Burn her!" Smith was immediately identified in the media as a modern-day Medea, an icon called forth every time a mother kills her child.

Euripides' Medea is a sorceress, a foreigner, and an experienced killer. When her husband leaves her for a younger, richer woman Medea kills their two sons and escapes in a winged chariot, leaving Jason helpless on the ground. An enigmatic and troubling figure in our cultural history, Medea reminds us that women are capable of murderous rage against those who depend upon them most. But was this suicidal twenty-three-year-old really a modern-day Medea?

Through the medium of television the nation watched the trial unfold. Cameras had captured the funeral and the burial of the two boys, and the anguished and angry faces of the public. Evening news programs showed images of that grieving public clutching teddy bears and laying wreaths at the site of the boys' drowning. But due to new legislation allowing cameras in the courtroom, the television audience also saw Susan Smith as she heard the charges read against her, and saw her eyes well up with tears when the prosecutor announced his intent to seek the death penalty. Though the judge later banned cameras from the courtroom in light of the media circus unfolding across the country at the O. J. Simpson trial, reporters still camped out at the courthouse door. There was never any doubt that Susan would be convicted; the dramatic questions at hand were 1) why did she do it? and 2) would she die for her crime? Prosecutors answered the first question by arguing that Susan Smith killed her sons because her new boyfriend didn't want children. Everyone waited for the jury to answer the second.

Television audiences, grown accustomed to seeing justice served in one-hour blocks, seemed poised to read the Smith trial as a familiar morality tale. The trial and guilty verdict would reassure an anxious public that Susan Smith was an aberration, an evil Lombrosian criminal who posed no threat to the institution of motherhood and the American family. But the old methods were losing their effectiveness. Though the initial impulse was to brand Smith as a self-centered monster, her trial revealed a complex portrait of a confused, depressed, and self-hating young woman. In the course of her trial it was revealed that Smith's father committed suicide when she was six, and her stepfather admitted to sexually abusing Susan beginning when she was fifteen. Psychologists linked this abuse to two suicide attempts made in her teens and to a period of hospitalization for severe depression. Her husband had left her for another woman soon after the birth of their second son, and she had recently been rejected by a man who viewed their relationship far more casually than Susan did.

The monstrous Medea turned out to be simply a deeply disturbed young woman who lacked any sense of self-worth. The authority figures in her life had all failed her, and her stepfather, who admitted to having sexually molested Susan as recently as three months before the murder, was the chair of the Union County Republican Party and the head of the South Carolina Christian Coalition. The easy lines of demarcation between good and evil, central to the morality tale form, were blurred beyond distinction and were ultimately useless in understanding why Alex and Michael died.

With its dramatic reversals and tragic outcome, the Susan Smith case seemed ideal for television coverage even though the more representative case would have been that of a father who killed his children. Though figures vary, studies show that approximately 70 to 80 percent of children killed by a parent are killed by their fathers.[2]

Though Smith's case was atypical, it spoke to a culture engaged in a fierce debate about women who leave their children to fend for themselves as they "selfishly" pursue their own desires. In an essay entitled "Murdering Mothers," Annalee Newitz explains that she is drawn to narratives about murderous mothers because "these stories are a way to murder the idea of 'mother' itself; they provide an escape route into another female identity entirely, one that does not inevitably head toward pregnancy and childrearing . . . [the killer mother] is a killer of tradition."[3] Though Newitz views this protest in a positive light, she is well within the minority.

A woman killing her two young sons spoke to a national anxiety about the decline of the American family and about a perceived lack of natural maternal self-sacrifice. Read on another level Smith could be a metaphor for the working mother who left her children in day care while she pursued a career. This same anxiety would be addressed in another popular television trial, or the case of *Commonwealth of Massachusetts v. Louise Woodward*.

The Nanny Murder Trial

By the end of the twentieth century traditional gender roles faced substantial challenges on psychological, legal, medical, and philosophical fronts, and many men and women were reconceiving their notions of gendered identity. In light of political and social advances for American women, one would expect a significant shift in the social and dramatic construction of the female criminal, and indeed the Susan Smith case heralded the decline of the simplistic binary of good woman/bad woman. But old habits die hard. The desire to contain the criminal woman in a narrative of monstrosity, so evident in the Ruth Snyder trial, has not yet been put to rest.

This chapter examines the trial of British au pair Louise Woodward for the murder of eight-month-old Matthew Eappen, one of the two children in her care. It was a case closely followed by the media, broadcast "gavel to gavel" on *Court TV,* and later used as the inspiration for an episode of the popular legal series *Law & Order.* The case was rife with ambiguity, from the coverage of the crime to the judge's eventual negation of the jury's verdict. Many of the themes that have emerged in previous chapters are evident in the Woodward case—the equation of womanhood with motherhood, the idealization of feminine self-sacrifice, and the perceived danger to cultural stability represented by the mother who works outside of her home. Though these centuries-old conceptions of gender emerge in the Woodward case, they seem to have lost some of their traction; the unanimous chorus of hatred that greeted Ruth Snyder has devolved into a complex fugue of point and counterpoint. In many ways the trial of Louise Woodward resisted narrative containment, though as a contemporary case study it both heartens and disturbs. The case and its subsequent representations both embrace and resist the cultural desire to disassociate the idealized woman from the criminal one and to criminalize the woman who steps outside traditional gender norms.

How did traditional gender norms contribute to the conviction of Louise Woodward for the murder of Matthew Eappen? On the surface they didn't. In keeping with the ambiguous response to this case, the discourse of female criminality was extended to indict the *victim,* or in this case, the victim's mother. The public debate over the responsibilities of working mothers became the focus of Woodward's defense lawyers who argued that Deborah Eappen be held morally, though not legally, responsible for Matthew's death because she had "neglected" her child when she returned to her part-time career as a doctor and left her children in the care of an au pair. The criminalization of the working mother became the central action in both the trial and in the dramatic retelling of the story on *Law & Order.* Despite many advances in women's legal and economic rights, the Woodward trial and public discourse surrounding it continued to play upon public fears of the disintegration of the American home in the face of changing gender expectations, fears first raised in the 1800s.

By the 1990s our culture had engaged in many debates about the moral and legal responsibilities of working mothers who place their role as family caregiver on par with or secondary to their role as economically independent agents. These debates evoke the arguments of antifeminist movements from the late nineteenth to the early twentieth century, arguments that held that a woman's primary role is to be wife and mother, the *femme couvert* who finds identity and purpose only when sacrificing her own needs to those of others. Though much has changed in light of the feminist movements of the twentieth century, the Woodward trial suggested that, as we enter the twenty-first century, we are still wrestling with an impulse to criminalize the woman who will not sublimate her own needs to those of her family.

During the last decade of the twentieth century, cable television became a staple of American entertainment. An increasingly popular component of cable programming is the televised trial, in which cameras record an actual trial in progress while anchors, modeling themselves on sports announcers, discuss the gains and losses of the respective sides.[4] The channel broadcasts twenty-four hours a day, seven days a week, with a majority of that time being devoted to live trial coverage. The very selection of a trial for coverage by the *Court TV* network codes it as one that merits national attention. As television critic Paul Thaler notes in his book *The Watchful Eye: American Justice in the Age of the Television Trial*, "the accused personifies the broader social issues attached to the case."[5] In the Woodward trial the broader social issue attached to the case against the au pair was a cultural unease about mothers in the workforce. When children are hurt while under the care of someone other than their parents the question inevitably arises: Where was the mother? These cases provide fodder for authors such as Danielle Crittenden, who would argue against women trying to balance motherhood and a career. In her best-selling book *What Our Mothers Didn't Tell Us: Why Happiness Eludes the Modern Woman* Crittenden argues that the 1970s feminists are to blame for much of the unhappiness and stress faced by working mothers today:

> My generation was raised to believe that by providing for our children's physical and material needs, we would compensate for the maternal comfort they lost by having us at work. Just so long as they were in "good care" we were told, we wouldn't have to worry about compromising our career. But this has proven to be a chimera: No amount of Fisher-Price geegaws, cheerfully painted walls, and chirping, brisk day care workers and nannies can replace a mother's love and attention.[6]

Crittenden blames feminism for luring women out of the home and into the workplace. Though the "traditional" two-parent, one income family is an historical anomaly, Crittenden holds it to be a norm from which we are deviating.

In 1999, 68 percent of mothers with children at home were in the labor force. Some of these women need to work and others work for reasons other than financial ones. These women rely on day care to provide a safe and nurturing environment for their children. Those who are financially well-off may even hire live-in nannies or engage young women to serve as au pairs. Such was the case with Deborah and Sunil Eappen.

On February 3, 1995, 911 operators received a frantic call from Louise Woodward saying that the infant in her care was cold and unresponsive. Matthew Eappen was brought to Boston's Children's Hospital, where doctors discovered retinal hemorrhages in each eye and a large subdural hematoma, which was causing pressure on the brain. Emergency surgery revealed extensive brain damage and internal hemorrhaging of the brain. Six days later Matthew Eappen died from fatal head injuries. An autopsy revealed a two-inch skull fracture in the back of his head and hemorrhages in the muscles of the baby's neck and spine. This indicated that the baby had been violently shaken for an extended period of time. Dr. Eli Newberger, director of the child protection team at Boston's Children's Hospital, said the child's injuries were so severe that the baby was probably shaken for at least sixty seconds before being struck against a hard object.[7]

The doctors agreed that Matthew Eappen was most likely the victim of SBS, or Shaken Baby Syndrome. SBS, which accounts for 10 to 12 percent of all deaths due to abuse and neglect in United States, is usually brought on when an adult shakes a child in an attempt to stop his or her inconsolable crying. Recent research on SBS shows that 80 percent of the perpetrators are male, most often the child's father or the mother's boyfriend. Six percent of the perpetrators are the mothers, and the remaining 14 percent are baby-sitters or day care workers (sex not specified).[8] When a baby is diagnosed as having been the victim of SBS there is an 80 percent chance that the person responsible was a male authority figure in the child's own home. In the Woodward trial, as with the Susan Smith trial, a crime that was a statistical anomaly became the focus of national attention through a televised trial. Though a baby would be much more likely to be injured or killed from severe shaking by a father or boyfriend, the national attention given to the Woodward case wrongly implied that the nation's young were at risk from the teenage baby-sitters and au pairs hired by women who wouldn't stay home with their own children.

The defense utilized this perception as it turned the focus of the trial away from the teenage defendant and onto Dr. Deborah Eappen. Playing "the working mom card" they attacked the infant's mother, arguing that her part-time work as an ophthalmologist resulted in her "neglecting" her family. *Court TV* broadcasted the hardball questioning of Dr. Deborah Eappen by defense attorney Barry Scheck, who contended that Dr. Eappen had failed in her responsibility to protect Matthew. This issue became the focus of a national debate. On the Internet, on call-in shows, in the tabloids, and in letters to the editor, Deborah Eappen became an unwitting defendant in the murder trial. In an interview with *The Nation*, she asked the interviewer, "How did Louise become the hero and I become the villain? . . . I strive in a lot of different directions in life, and suddenly that striving to be good seems to be bad."[9]

Web sites devoted to the trial were visited by thousands, and comments like the following could be found on AOL discussion boards and chat rooms:

> "She chose greed and not her children."
> "Deborah, absentee mother."
> "One less child, one more Volvo."
> "The face and actions of Deborah Eappen has me replaying Susan Smith over and over."[10]

The evocation of Susan Smith is telling; the case against Louise Woodward and the case against Susan Smith are completely dissimilar yet the two cases merged in the public mind because of the defense's strategy to frame Deborah Eappen as a selfish woman who put her own needs before her children's. Many who followed the case likened Deborah Eappen to Susan Smith, who had jeopardized the welfare of her children by putting her own needs before theirs. Just as these critics saw Smith sacrificing her children so she could be with a new boyfriend, they saw Eappen as sacrificing her child (not children, even though she had two) so that she could make money and enjoy the prestige of being a doctor. The most obvious flaw in the comparison was that Deborah Eappen was not the defendant in the case; Louise Woodward was.

Though Deborah Eappen was criticized in the court and in the press, the one-sided discourse of abnormality that had greeted Ruth Snyder was a thing of the past. Many came to Eappen's defense, pointing out the anachronistic, class- and race-biased reasoning of those who condemned her for working and at the same time called for the return of welfare mothers to the workforce. Journalist Katha Pollitt notes that Deborah Eappen is more than just a working mother, "she is a doctor, i.e., a woman with a man's job and to top it off a doctor's wife, thus a woman who doesn't 'need' to work. Obviously the whole thing must be her fault."[11] During the Woodward trial the *New York Times* ran a cartoon that captured the double standard being applied in the public criticism of Deborah Eappen. The cartoon consists of two panels. In the first panel two society women are looking at the newspaper headline "The Nanny Trial," and one says to the other, "How could that woman have left her children?" In the next panel the same two women pass a homeless woman and her children asking for money on the streets. They turn to her and say, "Why don't you get a job?!"

The cartoon reflects America's conflicted and inconsistent cultural response to working mothers. Much of the public concern with women who leave their children in the care of others while they work depends upon the class, and often race, of the mother in question. At the time of the Woodward trial Congress was passing sweeping welfare reforms that sent many single minority mothers into the workforce. In a *Salon* article entitled "Lessons of the Nanny Murder Trial," Dawn MacKeen writes, "We blame poor women for staying home with their children; they're considered good mothers if they go out and work instead of burdening the system with welfare dependency. Whereas middle-class and professional mothers are seen as bad for working."[12] The underlying message is that a woman should work only if she has to for financial reasons, and so it is not just any mom who should stay home with her children. Only the well-being of the middle-class white child is a line in the sand, a no compromise issue. Once again the traditional gender standard that defines "woman" as a caring and self-sacrificing mother is applied only to middle- and upper-class white women.

The defense had put Deborah Eappen on trial, and the lawyers were so confident of their case that the defense insisted the jury consider only the case of murder. They felt that if manslaughter was an option the jury would probably take it, but if they had to say that Louise Woodward committed murder they would most likely acquit. The gamble didn't pay off. *Court TV* audiences around the country watched the jury deliver a verdict of guilty of murder in the second degree. Cameras recorded the stunned face of Louise Woodward and the devastated and angry faces of her friends and relatives watching the trial on television in England. A Woodward supporter posted the following message on one of the Woodward trial Web sites: "Behind this case lies the fact that the American middle class dream is carried on the shoulders of millions like Louise Woodward, inexperienced nannies imported from abroad as cheap labour for parents who want the kids and a two car lifestyle. For the jury to find Woodward innocent would have meant a guilty verdict against the risky choices made by the majority of American parents."[13]

But the trial had a surprise ending, which left the issue of Deborah Eappen and Louise Woodward's relative guilt unresolved. In a very unusual move, Judge Zobel decided to release his sentencing judgment over the Internet. The full text of his decision was available to the wired world, and when it was released several million people logged on to read it. Zobel upset the prosecutor's victory by ostensibly overturning the jury's verdict. Though Louise was technically still guilty of murder in the second degree, she was sentenced only to time served and released on her own recognizance. The judge's stunning *deus ex machina* had all the characteristics of a scripted conclusion to a courtroom drama. Unlike previous cases that were resolved by a verdict, this one, and the social issues attached to it, seemed to resist closure, refusing to be contained in the traditional courtroom narrative. Louise was guilty but wouldn't be punished. As she boarded the British Airways flight back to England, images of Medea escaping the wrath of Jason in a winged chariot came to mind.

Prime-Time Law

The televised trial and the subsequent televised retellings of it represent the latest incarnation of the narrative containment of female criminality. Its predecessors, the ballads, dramas, and television movies of the week, were stable narratives constructed only once (though endlessly performed) and from a central point of view. *Court TV* and the plethora of legal dramas, reenactments, and television series that constitute today's legal narratives are multivocal, presenting diverse perspectives on the nature of crime, guilt, and innocence. With these multiple levels of representation, the lines between the televised trial, the documentary reenactments, and the scripted television movies are not always easy to maintain. For many viewers the separate forms begin to seep into each other, giving the fictional narratives more authority while at the same time coding the actual trial as public entertainment.

Like the crime ballads, melodramas, and social conscience plays before them, the television legal drama, as distinct from the televising of actual courtrooms, has become a site in which anxieties over cultural disruptions may be contained in a carefully constructed crime narrative. In the earlier forms the story would end with the criminal or disruptive woman tried and punished, but many of the contemporary legal televisions dramas resist easy closure and problematize the very notion of justice, guilt, and innocence. One such television series is *Law & Order*, created by Dick Wolf in 1990 and still highly rated at the time of this writing. The show is known for taking on topical issues that have surfaced in actual trials. Very often the television episode based upon an actual case is broadcast within weeks of the original trial. It was inevitable that the Woodward trial would become a subject of this popular series.

Law & Order follows a two-part formula in which the first half of the program is devoted to the police identifying and arresting a suspect, while the second half follows the lawyers in the district attorney's office as they seek a conviction. The show is known for bringing the workings of the legal system into conflict with the assumption that truth is revealed in the courtroom, and episodes often revolve around the question "What is the real crime here?"

Though the series often destabilizes conventional notions of a guilt/innocence binary, a consistent theme in the series is the insistence that someone be held accountable for harmful actions. In this manner it is no different from its predecessors, the ballad and the melodrama. However, *Law & Order* expands the notion of responsibility to include both remote and immediate causes of crime, often scrutinizing society at large, its culture, history, prejudice, privilege, and poverty as potential sources of criminal motivation. Past forms of the crime narrative, such as ballads and melodramas, almost always assigned blame to an individual, neglecting the larger contextual reasons for the criminal action.

On another level the series demystifies the law by showing it to be constructed, sometimes arbitrarily, and always open to new interpretation. *Law & Order* questions the very notion of crime as a stable category, and as its characters debate different positions in a given case the series projects a message that the law is constantly in negotiation. Still, since it is the police, lawyers, and judges engaged in debating whether a crime did or did not occur, the series also asserts that those who determine the criminality of an action are in privileged positions.

By showing that lawyers and judges and juries can use the law to effect social justice or to reinscribe and enforce social injustice, the courtroom is presented as a potential arena for change. Many of the plots revolve around the negotiations that must take place when a private sense of justice comes into conflict with the Law. When the series adapts the events of an actual criminal case, such as that of Louise Woodward, its format allows characters to debate the social issues attached to the source trial.

The case of Louise Woodward sparked debates about the responsibility, or lack thereof, of mothers who leave their children in the care of others. Using this trial as a basis for an episode entitled "Homesick," the writers of *Law & Order* changed a number of details but kept the defense's attack on the victim's mother as the central dramatic action. The title evokes the notion of missing one's home and family, but it resonates on many other levels as well. It can evoke the image of a child longing for its mother or the image of getting sick at home, in the one place where you should be safest. The episode also engages the viewer in an examination of the home as patient—implying that the home itself may be ailing and headed for demise if it is not cured soon.

"Homesick"

The episode opens with a businessman telling a cabby to wait while he rushes in to say hello to his new baby before running back to work. He is greeted by Lila, a British au pair, and then runs up to the nursery to see his son. When he finds the baby cold and unresponsive he rushes to the hospital, where the baby is pronounced dead. The mother, in a business suit, briefcase in hand, rushes into the emergency room, too late to see her baby alive. She is clearly coded through costume as an executive, working woman, and her absence in the story up to this point is tied to her job outside of the home.

As the detectives try to find out why the baby died it is revealed that another au pair had a baby die in her care. In a provocative scripting choice this baby's name was Matthew, mentioned twice in passing but evoking the still-fresh memory of Matthew Eappen. Later, the district attorney refers to a Swiss nanny who was acquitted in a murder trial, leaving the impression that there is an outbreak of babies dying at the hands of negligent nannies while mothers are out working.

The detectives seem to see the parents as, at least partially, responsible for the baby's death, and they exchange numerous cracks about how the Karmels were "very doting parents when their schedules permitted." As in the Woodward trial, a class bias is implied in the detectives' criticism. The detectives' boss is a working mother, and they see no problem with that; it is the lack of the victim's mother's financial "need" to work that bothers them in this case.

The investigation reveals that the parents had arguments and that the forty-eight-year-old father, on his second marriage, was angry at his twenty-seven-year-old wife for working twelve-hour days. The delivery boy testifies he heard the mother yelling back at the father, "You wanted the damn baby. You stay home and wipe his ass!" The sense that the mother is uninterested in her child or his death is heightened when the detectives find her back at her job the day after the baby's death. When they remark on their surprise the mother becomes defensive:

> DET. BRISCOE: You must have had this kind of a situation right along. I mean the conflict between work and childraising.
> MRS. KARMEL: Oh, I see. Women should be barefoot and in the kitchen.
> DET. BRISCOE: I didn't hear me say that.
> MRS. KARMEL: We hired Lila to help us through that conflict. Why are we talking about this?

Why are they talking about this? In this episode the police captain, doctor, coroner, psychiatrist, defense attorney, assistant district attorney, jury foreperson, and judge are all women. Their participation in the workforce is never questioned; rather it is portrayed as unexceptional and completely natural. The detectives interact with all of these professional women on a regular basis; the suggestion that childrearing and work are in conflict is only raised with the victim's mother. Presumably, the audience is meant to notice the inconsistency.

After questioning the mother at work, suspicion turns to Lila, the au pair, when the detectives learn that she was fired from her previous job. When they interview the former employer, the woman says they let Lila go because she wanted to stay home and take care of her baby. She felt that Lila didn't really bond with the child. Her husband had been more suspicious and had installed secret cameras in hopes of catching Lila treating the infant roughly. The tapes revealed no abuse but, the mother says, no great enthusiasm either. Throughout the scene she is occupied feeding the baby. In clear contrast to Mrs. Karmel, this young mother desires to be at home with her baby and believes that there is no substitute for a mother's care.

The two scenes emphasize the contrast in the daily lives of the two young mothers—Mrs. Karmel's office is elegant, bright, and spacious, with a panoramic view of New York City. Throughout the interview with the detectives she stands and they sit in the visitor chairs. The mother who gave up her job to take care of her child is in a dimly lit, cluttered, somewhat claustrophobic space, and she kneels or sits by the baby as the detectives stand over her. Individual characters in the episode may romanticize the stay-at-home mother or demonize the career woman, but the overall episode doesn't appear to elevate one over the other.

The detectives begin to focus on Lila when her former boyfriend describes her dislike of the baby in her charge. The detectives question Lila, asking why she didn't respond when Matthew cried all morning, and she explodes, saying, "I'm not his mother! I came here be an art student not a bloody wet nurse! Look, I did the best I could." When they discover a pesticide in her room that matches the poison ingested by the baby, Lila is arrested and charged with murder. A diary recording her dislike of the baby appears to add motive to the case. This is the "closure" of the investigative portion of the episode.

At the midpoint of the episode several themes emerge. The two male detectives feel that the parents, in particular the mother, were at fault for being away from the baby so much. The references to other cases by doctors and lawyers imply that the death of children under a baby-sitter's care is a growing and prevalent problem in the metropolitan area. And finally, it is made clear that the nanny was neither trained for nor interested in childcare. Since we never see any other au pair to balance the picture, the implication is that Lila is typical of all au pairs: low paid, homesick, and resentful of the family that exploits them at a hundred dollars a week. It is interesting to note that these characteristics were all raised in the Woodward trial.

As the episode shifts into the legal section the issues of guilt and responsibility are explored in more depth. Though the judge and the defense lawyer are women, the detectives who arrested Lila and the lawyer who will prosecute her are all men. Jack McCoy, representing the state of New York, is the lead prosecutor on the case, though he is assisted by a female lawyer, Claire Kincaid. Convinced of Lila's guilt, McCoy points out that she was untrained, isolated, depressed, and homesick, and he calls an expert witness to show that these characteristics in caretakers have been associated with violence toward children. The implication that we are using outdated perceptions to judge contemporary situations is neatly introduced when the defense attorney points out that the studies quoted by the "expert" were done in Germany nearly eighty years ago. In a later scene the two women attorneys will also put the case into a historical context when Claire Kincaid accuses the defense attorney of "setting feminism back fifty years" with her attack on the victim's mother.

In what is structurally the center of the episode Ruth Miller, Lila's defense attorney, mirrors Barry Scheck in the Woodward trial when she interrogates Mrs. Karmel on the stand. She blames the mother for not researching the agency or Lila herself and for not spending any time at home. She compliments the mother for having a rich husband at which point the mother defensively replies, "I see where you are going with this and I think it is disgusting." Over continued objections from the prosecutor, Miller reduces the mother to tears when she asks her how many naps her son took and what his favorite toy was. McCoy objects often but the judge allows the questioning. Two separate close-ups on Claire Kincaid show her discomfort with the defense attorney's strategy. The judge finally silences Miller when she says that the mother was "constantly, unnecessarily and selfishly flitting about the country. She wouldn't know if O. J. was taking tea in her kitchen." The defense attorney is asking the jury to blame the victim for letting the criminal into the home.

The next scene is an informal meeting between the two female attorneys. As Ruth Miller walks into the diner, Claire Kincaid turns to her and says, "Nice show today." This is a moment worth exploring in detail. The implication that the whole attack on the mother was a show raises the question, Who was the show for? Obviously the jury. This suggests that a jury, like a television or theater audience, is swayed by a dramatic narrative that needs only the appearance of truth. In fact, when the actual truth is complex and self-contradictory, juries/audiences feel more comfortable if the situation is reduced to a black-and-white one with clearly defined villains and innocent victims. Relying on traditional, if inaccurate, gender expectations, Miller reframes the villain in the case, shifting blame from the nanny to the mother.

The dialogue that follows is revealing because it is the point at which the episode's central issue—the disapproval of working mothers—is articulated and argued between two working women. I quote it at length:

CLAIRE: You made her look like Lizzie Borden in there.
RUTH: Lizzie Borden whacks her family and becomes a feminist cause celebre. . . .
CLAIRE: And Wendy Karmel doesn't and you use her to set feminism back fifty years.
RUTH: Because I showed how negligent she was.
CLAIRE: Because you played on the misconception held by one half of that jury.
RUTH: Oh, I see. You think work and family are both entitlements of women?
CLAIRE: It's a personal choice. You work. You have a kid.
RUTH: Do you think I'd be doing this if Martin didn't run off with his dentist?
CLAIRE: Wild horses couldn't drag you out of the courtroom. I don't think your five-year-old stands a chance.

Barry Scheck's defense of the au pair relied heavily on his criticism of the mother, and that aspect of the case received much of the national attention. This scene in *Law & Order* shows two professional women engaged in that same debate. But it is important to note that the debate occurs outside of the courtroom—that is to say it does not and will not affect the outcome of the trial—and occurs only in the private conversation of two women. The series often explores different sides of controversial issues by having attorneys argue them in the courtroom scenes, but this episode never allows the defense attorney's (feigned?) bias against working women to be rebutted in court. The legal implications of the social prejudice remain unchallenged within the legal system, and Claire, who articulates the feminist response, is significantly silent in the active, result-producing arena of the courtroom. The episode offers the possibility of a feminist jurisprudence but implies that it exists at a theoretical level only; we are not yet ready to put it into action in the courtroom.

When the episode moves back into the courtroom, the jury forewoman concedes that the jury is deadlocked, seven to five, against conviction. The dialogue reflects that it was the mother's testimony that made them question Lila's guilt. A mistrial is declared, but when McCoy announces his plans to go to trial again, District Attorney Adam Schiff, the voice of authority and experience (who is never seen arguing a case), tells him to give it up. Claire says, "On retrial we'll pick a more enlightened jury." Schiff responds, "Find me twelve citizens who think a woman's place is closing deals in Chicago."

The series is known for surprise endings, and this episode is no exception. While reprepping one of the prosecution witnesses, the father's son by his first marriage, Claire discovers that the half-brother actually poisoned the baby. When he is questioned by the judge the boy says he was angry because his father, obsessed with his new family, had forgotten to take him to a Yankees game. McCoy asks, "You killed Evan because [your father] forgot?" The boy replies, "He forgot everything. . . . I'm supposed to be his son too you know." In a strange twist on the Medea story, the child, abandoned by his father, kills his infant rival. While all the attention had been focused on the mother's responsibility to her child, the cause of the crime is laid at the feet of the father who reneged on his responsibilities to his child.

In the end the episode suggests that both Lila and Mrs. Karmel were put on trial (one officially and one unofficially) because they did not possess the maternal instincts deemed an essential characteristic of an innocent woman. The story line seems to follow Lombrosian criminological reasoning, implying that a woman who is not selflessly devoted to children is a guilty woman. Though no character bluntly articulates this nineteenth-century pseudoscientific position, the episode neatly builds a sexist narrative that places two women on trial for not loving a baby enough. The fact that the actual killer is a young boy denied his *father's* love, explodes the Lombrosian construction and reveals the danger of relying on outmoded gender expectations in the courtroom.

In her book *Prime Time Law* Dawn Keetley offers this potent analysis of the episode's final twist: "That a *father's* absence from his family, due to his absorption in not only his career but also a new family, can be the remote cause of a crime is a truth investigators and jurors may be blinded to, the episode suggests, if they see only the disingenuous and sexist narrative condemning working *mothers* spun by the defense lawyer in her attempt to exonerate her client."[14]

This study has demonstrated how representations of female criminality are shaped into gendered morality tales that *circulate* through the courts, the newspapers, television, and the theater. It has also examined how these morality tales feed into (and on) a cultural discourse of gender by criminalizing women who step outside of the conventional gender norm of the self-sacrificing wife and mother, and assert their independence and right to self-actualization. Though we have come a long way since Alice Arden was burned at the stake, "Homesick" requires us to acknowledge the power that nineteenth-century gender expectations continues to exert over twentieth-century juries. Unless we can dismantle the age-old narratives that equate the independent woman with the criminal woman, we must accept that gendered stereotypes may still blind us in our search for justice.

chapter 6

narratives of resistance

Feminist theorists of theatre turned insistently to consider how ideology was embedded in texts and performances, how spectators were positioned to accept such ideologies unquestioningly, how feminists might best come to understand texts and performances in order to subvert them, and how performances might contribute to the disruption of such ideologies.[1]

WHEN MEDEA FIRST walked on the stage in fifth-century B.C. Athens, she was not a woman at all; she was a man in a mask speaking the words of a male playwright to a gathering of male citizens. Embedded in her story and embodied in his figure was the fear that women might begin to act like men, putting their own needs first and raging against those who would oppress them by denying them their individual complexity. Since her first appearance Medea has given birth to many angry, complex, and rebellious women, five of whose stories have appeared so far in this book. In the past five hundred years the anxiety provoked by Medea's daughters has been dissipated by enveloping them in legal and dramatic narratives of containment, most often authored by male lawyers, juries, and playwrights, narratives that defeminize them and divide them from other women. Like Medea, they are portrayed as the foreigners, the "non" women. As the cases of Alice Arden, Mary Edmondson, Ruth Snyder, Francine Hughes, and Louise Woodward have demonstrated, to read how these murderous women were represented in the legal and dramatic discourse of their time is to learn what acceptable female behavior was in their culture. In this essentialist criminology, no woman adhering to the gender expectations of the culture can ever be convicted of murder. If she is found innocent she will be shown to be a reasonable woman and a dutiful wife/daughter/mother. If she is found guilty, she will be shown to be deviant, no longer a member of woman-class, but spawned from some depraved criminal class, the embodied antithesis of femininity.

In the legal and dramatic narratives examined here, Alice Arden becomes a manipulative, oversexed adulteress; Mary Edmondson is defeminized in the ballads by emphasizing her masculine appearance and her lack of housekeeping inclinations; Ruth Snyder becomes monstrous, and Francine Hughes must be recast in the body of an angel before we can forgive her crimes. Finally, Deborah Eappen, who was never the defendant to begin with, becomes the accused when she seems to put her own career in front of her children's needs. Though the narratives do their best to defeminize and ostracize these female murderers from all other women, the implicit fear is there: Gentlemen, watch your wives and daughters, for they too could turn on you in anger.

Though isolating and controlling the woman who kills through legal and dramatic narratives has been effective, there have been occasional resistant voices. Judith Butler writes that "gender is in no way a stable identity or a locus of agency from which various acts proceed; rather, it is an identity tenuously constituted in time—an identity instituted through a *stylized repetition of acts*" (emphasis mine).[2] If, as Butler argues, gender is instituted through a repetition of acts, theater (most certainly "a stylized repetition of acts") has the potential to become a powerful tool of resistance and transformation. By instituting what Butler calls "a different sort of repeating," constrictive gender ideology can be rethought and reenacted.[3]

In 1928 Sophie Treadwell's *Machinal* presented a different sort of repeating by using expressionist techniques to show Ruth Snyder's crimes through her own eyes, not the eyes of the male-dominated culture that judged her. Furthermore, she undermined the standard tactic of distancing the criminal woman from the "normal" women of the country by stating in the beginning of the play that her unnamed Young Woman is "every woman."[4] Two contemporary plays, like Treadwell's 1928 play, should be considered narratives of resistance: Sharon Pollock's *Blood Relations* and Dario Fo and Franca Rame's *Medea*. This chapter shows how each presents feminist alternatives to patriarchal containment of the rebellious woman. They neither make a heroine out of their "murderess" nor do they excuse her, but like Treadwell in *Machinal* they offer a feminist perspective on what prompted the woman to violent response. Each play also foregrounds the act of representation. Unlike the Arden or Hughes narratives, which try to present their interpretation of the historical event as unproblematic documentary, each of these plays acknowledges the feminist perspective of its creator. I will end where I began—with the staged body of Medea—but first there is a woman who has been waiting in the wings; though never convicted of a crime she is still perhaps the most famous American murderess.

Blood Relations

What American does not know that Lizzie Borden took an axe, gave her mother forty whacks, and when she saw what she had done, she gave her father forty-one? The fact that Lizzie Andrew Borden was acquitted of the murder of her father and stepmother in August 1893 is quite beside the point; legend has made her a murderess in spite of the historical outcome of her case. She is now part of American folklore, and her legend is the source for at least two operas, a ballet, eight plays, a television movie, a film, poems, songs, novels, and of course a children's rhyme.

Representations of Lizzie Borden must confront the ambiguous outcome of her case; in fact, the ambiguity forces us to acknowledge the power that representation played in constructing her as the quintessential American murderess. Lizzie Borden never testified at her trial; the legal and journalistic record of her case relies entirely upon other people's interpretation of her actions and motives. There is no confession, no denial, no "authentic" voice to confirm or complicate the legend; Lizzie never revealed a thing, and so each of us in turn has filled her silence with our own desire for coherence.

Canadian playwright Sharon Pollock's *Blood Relations*, set ten years after the trial, foregrounds the generative force of representation in the life and afterlife of Lizzie Borden. In the first version of the play (originally entitled *My Name Is Lizbeth*), Sharon Pollock wrote a linear narrative in which she confirmed the popular, if not legal, acceptance of Lizzie's guilt. In this version the narrative was closed, doubt was erased, and coherence assured. But Pollock realized that it was the doubt, the distrust of coherence that fascinated her. So she wrote another play.

Blood Relations is set ten years after Lizzie's acquittal, and though the forty-two-year-old Lizzie Borden appears in the play, the thirty-two-year-old "Lizzie," the woman accused of patricide, is actually created onstage by the character of the Actress. Though unnamed, this actress is clearly Nance O'Neil, the Boston tragedienne rumored to have been Lizzie's lover. In *Blood Relations* it is through the Actress's body, with its attendant desires and fears, that "Lizzie Borden" reenacts her "crime." Through the character of the Actress, Pollock does exactly what the attorneys in the original case did—-she speaks for a defendant who never spoke for herself. But whereas the male attorneys, judge, and jury constructed a narrative of containment around the trial of Lizzie Borden, Pollock creates a narrative of feminist resistance.

The Legal Narrative of Containment

Lizzie Borden's defense was built on and in fact depended on the belief that the gentlemen of the jury shared common assumptions about women and how they behave. If the jury believed the defense's representation of

narratives of resistance

Lizzie as a true woman, that is to say, a woman who spent her life devoted to others, they could not find her guilty of murder. As long as they were convinced that Lizzie was both dependent upon her father and fulfilled in her daughterly love, gender ideology would outweigh the physical evidence and she would be acquitted. Lizzie's attorney told the jury that to find her guilty they would have to reach outside of human experience to justify the verdict:

> It is not impossible that a good person may go wrong. But our human experience teaches us that if a daughter grows up in one of our homes to be 32 years old, educated in our schools, walking in our streets, associating with the best people and devoted to the service God and man, binding up the wounds of the unfortunate, teaching the ignorant and down-trodden, spending her life for others, it is not within human experience to find her suddenly come out into the rankest and baldest murderess. *That would be a condition of things so contrary to all that our human life has taught us that our hearts and feelings revolt at the conception.*[5] (Emphasis mine)

The district attorney in the case said that "It is hard, it is hard to *conceive* that woman can be guilty of crime."[6] A rather broad statement to be sure, but in her excellent analysis of the Borden case, Ann Jones indicates why the jury might find it inconceivable for a "real" woman, as they understood the category "woman," to be a murderess:

> Lizzie owed her life largely to those tacit assumptions: ladies aren't strong enough to swing a two-pound hatchet hard enough to break a brittle substance one-sixteenth of an inch thick. Ladies cry a lot. Ladies love to stay home all the time. Ladies are ceaselessly grateful to the men—fathers or husbands—who support them. Ladies never stand with their legs apart. Ladies cannot plan more than a few minutes ahead. Ladies [sic] conversation arises from ignorance, hysteria, over-enthusiasm, or the inability to use language properly, and in any case, is not to be taken seriously.[7]

None of these tacit assumptions applied, however, to servant women, foreign women, lesbian women, or any other women who stepped outside the bounds of class and gender expectations. The only other person in the house at the time of the murders, and hence the only other possible suspect, was Bridget Sullivan, the Borden's Irish maid. Both her class and her nationality made her vulnerable, but fortunately for her, she was able to provide an alibi that could not be shaken by the defense. The prosecutor, District Attorney Knowlton, addressed the issue of class in his summation:

> One woman [Bridget] is poor and friendless, a domestic, a servant, uneducated and without friends, and the other [Lizzie] is buttressed by all that social rank and wealth and friends and counsel can do for her protection . . . supposing those things that have been suggested against Lizzie Borden had been found against Bridget Sullivan, poor friendless girl. . . . Is there one law for Bridget and another for Lizzie?[8]

The answer, of course was yes. Lizzie was a "gentlewoman," the daughter of one of the most prominent families in southeastern Massachusetts, educated, churchgoing, associating with "the best people." Certainly, had a scrap of evidence been found against Bridget, she would have been tried and convicted before you could say, "no Irish need apply."

As discussed in chapter 2, in the nineteenth century the prosecution would attempt to show that the female defendant possessed "criminal" characteristics, that is, motives, appearance, or behaviors that subverted the ideal construction of womanhood. Conversely, the defense would emphasize the woman's willing acceptance of culturally sanctioned, class appropriate gender roles. Lizzie Borden was protected by her status as the daughter of one of Fall River's leading businessmen, as a young woman who taught Sunday school and worked for the Ladies Temperance Society. As a result the prosecution was unable to draw on the usual discourses of abnormality, traditionally so useful against women defendants.

Though the prosecution never questioned Lizzie's femininity, the press at first drew upon the discourses of gender abnormality, defeminizing Lizzie's appearance. Upon her arrest she was described in the press as having "thick protruding lips, pallid from sickness, and a mouth drawn down into very deep creases that denote either a melancholy or an irritable disposition . . . her jaws are strong and conspicuous."[9] To counter this image created by the press of Lizzie as a "pallid, sickly, jowly, irritable *woman*," the defense refigured her as a "defenseless *girl*," a "damsel in distress." She was a dutiful daughter, twice victimized, tried for her life as she mourned the loss of her protector. No matter that she was a thirty-two-year-old, able-bodied woman; as represented by counsel, she was a girl: virginal, silent, dependent, and incapable of her own defense. It was an effective strategy. The criminal had become the victim. The same papers that had called her jowly and pallid now wrote that "there is nothing wicked, criminal, or hard in her features."[10] That a murderess would have monstrous features stood unchallenged; the defendant was transformed to accommodate the defense.

The defense attorney made the implications of finding Lizzie guilty very clear to the twelve men on the jury. "Gentlemen. To find Lizzie Borden guilty you must believe that she is a fiend. Does she look it? The prisoner at the bar is a Christian woman, the equal of your wife and mine."[11] If Lizzie was a "normal woman" *and* an axe murderer, then every man in Fall River must look to his own wife and daughter with suspicion. As Ann Jones says of the case, "surely it is preferable under such circumstances not to punish the offender but to pretend there has been no offense."[12] And that is precisely what happened; the court's desire for Lizzie to be incapable of the crime was so strong that it overshadowed the physical evidence. Lizzie was acquitted, the case was closed, and no attempt was ever made to find the murderer.

After inheriting her father's fortune, Lizzie changed her name to Lizbeth and moved into a mansion on "the hill," which she called Maplecroft. One year after the murder an editorial ran in the Providence *Journal*. "There is no reason now for Miss Borden's silence; let her speak! Let her spare no effort to bring this horrible case to a more satisfactory conclusion." Lizzie, now Lizbeth, ignored the call for an explanation and remained silent, and the public, which had rallied to her defense, began to turn against her. Perhaps had she faded gracefully into obscurity, teaching Sunday school, having tea with ladies of similar quality, or even marrying, legend would not have made her the axe murderer she became. But the pretension of changing her name and flaunting her wealth did not sit well with her community, and the recriminations and recriminalization of Lizzie began.

Though Lizzie and her sister Emma rarely ventured into the town of Fall River, Lizzie did begin traveling to Boston quite frequently in order to attend the theater. She admired the Boston actress Nance O'Neil, and she sought out a friendship with her. Rumors of a lesbian affair with the actress began to circulate as Lizzie's trips to Boston increased. When it was discovered that she had loaned Nance money for a down payment on a new home, suspicions seemed confirmed. Nance was a frequent guest at Maplecroft, and it was rumored that a huge party thrown for the actress and her company had convinced Emma Borden to leave her sister and move out of Fall River.

Lizzie was found innocent because she was an upper-class woman whose lawyers represented her as a defenseless girl, a dutiful daughter and a good Christian. She was recriminalized when she refused to adhere to the same image that freed her. The same people who had once defended her now called her a "witch" and an "uppity spinster," and they accused her of being a drunk and a lesbian. It is unclear whether people thought her guilty because her behavior had changed or whether they had always thought her guilty and were simply expressing their belief that she had "gotten away with murder" by reapplying the discourse of abnormality in retrospect.

Re-presenting Lizzie Borden: The Resistant Theatrical Narrative

Pollock's final version of the play begins with a woman reciting Hermione's defense from *Winter's Tale*: "Since what I am about to say must be but that which contradicts my accusation, and the testimony on my part no other but what comes from myself, it shall scarce boot me to say, "Not Guilty" (14).[13] Called only the Actress, this is Nance O'Neil, the woman whose name was linked to Lizzie's by the Fall River gossips. Pollock writes her play in the negotiated space between the two women, and the power dynamics in their relationship, ten years after the fact, become the ground upon which we witness the murder of Andrew and Abigail Borden.

In the first scene, as the two women waltz together, the Actress tells Miss Lizzie that she *needs* to know, "Did she or didn't she?" Lizzie's answer is characteristically enigmatic.

> MISS LIZZIE: Why is it important?
> THE ACTRESS: I have a compulsion to know the truth.
> MISS LIZZIE: The truth? Sometimes I think you look like me and you're not jowly.
> THE ACTRESS: No.
> MISS LIZZIE: You look like me, or how I think I look, or how I ought to look . . . sometimes you think like me . . . do you feel that?
> THE ACTRESS: Sometimes.
> MISS LIZZIE: *Triumphant.* You shouldn't have to ask then. You should know. "Did I, didn't I." You tell me. (19–20)

Instead of telling the Actress "the truth," Miss Lizzie draws her into a reenactment of the event, a reenactment in which Miss Lizzie plays the family's maid, Bridget, and the Actress assumes the role of Lizzie. In the text Lizzie's two character names appear juxtaposed: she becomes Miss Lizzie/Bridget, while the Actress loses her own identity and becomes simply Lizzie.

First Lizzie describes the maid Bridget to the Actress, then she begins to imitate her testimony on the stand. As "Bridget" describes the Borden household to "the court," the Bordens begin to appear on the stage while the Actress watches. Miss Lizzie/Bridget turns to the Actress and speaks to her as if she were Lizzie. From that point on the Actress begins to create the role of "Lizzie Borden." The transformation, tentative at first, soon seems natural. As the Actress begins to see the events through her own working-woman's perspective, what results is an economic explanation for the murder. In the Actress's re-presentation, Lizzie's father is about to deed the family property over to his wife, leaving his daughters dependent on the stepmother they loathe. Lizzie's only other option, if she is to be free of her stepmother's economic control, is to marry a local widower who is in need of a wife. After all, as her father points out, a thirty-two-year-old woman must not expect to be choosy. When her father says Johnny MacLeod is looking for a wife, Lizzie (as played now by the Actress) shoots back, "No god damn it, he's looking for a housekeeper and it isn't going to be me!" (39)

By the beginning of the second act, the Actress realizes that she is starting to control the story and that she no longer needs prompting from Miss Lizzie/Bridget; once in control of the narrative she begins to plot the murder of Abigail. She asks the family doctor: if two people were dying and he could save only one, wouldn't he decide that the younger one should live? Are not some lives more important than others? Lizzie rationalizes the death of her stepmother—after all, "You put poison out for the slugs in your garden" (62). Under the economic rule of Abigail, Lizzie will have no hope of transformation, no life of her own; one way or another, one of them must die. And so Lizzie kills in "self-defense," literally to maintain her sense of self.

Once the story has played itself out and the murders have been committed, the Actress turns to Miss Lizzie, triumphant at "discovering" the truth:

> THE ACTRESS: Lizzie . . . Lizzie, you did. *(She takes the hatchet from Miss Lizzie)*
> MISS LIZZIE: I didn't. (The Actress looks to the hatchet—then to the audience) You did. (70)

When Lizzie says "I didn't. You did" she is speaking as much to the audience as to the Actress. We are implicated in the final gesture of the play— we have taken the representation for truth and in doing so, have made it so. The representation of the criminal woman (whether it be on stage, in the press, or in the courts) is inextricably linked to her historical identity, and Pollock shows how easily that identity can be constructed from our own desires and fears. *Blood Relations* decenters the celebrity subject, using the exchange of roles to foreground the fact that we are witnessing an interpretation of the event and not the event itself. Of course, this is actually happening on two levels: while the Actress plays Lizzie, another actress (a real one), plays Miss Lizzie, who in turn plays Bridget the maid. One actress is no more authentic than the other, but the Lizzie created by the character of the Actress is the one we begin to believe, and her representation of the crime remains our strongest image of the event. *Blood Relations* foregrounds the role representation played in creating an image of "Lizzie Borden" only loosely connected to its historical subject. In this play Pollock exposes the ideology behind the act of representation that is central to the narrative containment of the criminal woman.

Blood Relations's ambiguous ending resists the closure that all other interpretations of the Borden story, most specifically the legal interpretation, insisted upon. By using the transference of identity Pollock disrupts the coherence of the narrative, and in so doing attacks the cultural expectations that code the female as stable, unable to transform, hence as ultimately controllable. Pollock resists closure, not simply because it is a rebellious act but because the ideas of closure and coherence have been traditionally used against women, and as a battered wife she knows this. She writes the following in her introduction to the play:

> Prior to working in the theatre, I was married for some years to a violent man. I spent a great deal of time devising, quite literally, murderous schemes to rid me of him. I implemented none of them for none of them struck me as suitably foolproof. Eventually, I crept, with my children, into the night when it was forcibly brought home to me that in all likelihood, I was cast as the murderee, not the murderer in my drama . . . I would not have killed for money and real estate, I would not have killed to prevent injury to myself . . . I would have killed to maintain my sense of self, to prevent a violation that was far more frightening and threatening than any blow, and of which physical violence against my person was only the outward manifestation. And so it was with Lizzie.[14]

Here is another narrative of desire through which Lizzie Borden is re-presented to us. Pollock's desire for Lizzie's frustration and pain to be like her own ("so it was with Lizzie") is, like the Actress's longing for Lizzie to be a materialist feminist, merely the inscription of the representer's desire on the body of the historical subject. In a sense it is a mirror of what happened in the courtroom when the silent Lizzie was represented by lawyers who invested her with their own desire for her to be a dutiful daughter of the patriarchy. Implied in that desire was their fear of the alternative; to allow her to be anything else was to give her a power they would never relinquish.

Whether or not Lizzie Borden took an axe, the token acts assigned to her are suffused with narratives of desire. The court represented Lizzie as the dutiful daughter they desired her to be. Through Nance O'Neill, Pollock represents Lizzie as the rebel and avenger she hoped to be in her own life. Using the power of dramatic representation, patriarchal culture has been successful in containing women in a binary discourse of womanhood, where the "good woman" is self-sacrificing and the "criminal woman" is self-serving. In *Blood Relations* Pollock shows how the power of representation can just as effectively be used to resist binary assumptions as it can to reinforce them.

While Pollock makes us aware of the ideologies behind representations, Italian playwrights/actors Dario Fo and Franca Rame take resistance to another level. They begin, like Pollock, by revealing the ideology that lies behind the defeminization of the criminal woman and the subsequent criminalization of the feminist woman. But they also actively subvert that ideology through the power of resistant performance. Fo and Rame offer a radical interpretation of the Medea legend in a set of monologues entitled *Female Parts* (in Italian *Tutta casa, letto e chiesa*, All home, work and church).[15] Political satirists Fo and Rame retell canonized stories of Western culture through a Marxist lens. In their retelling they challenge our assumptions about the historical validity of our most central narratives. Fo has said his paradoxical narratives were "a sacred refusal to accept the logic of convention; a rebellion against the moral assumption that always sees the good on one side and the bad always and only on the other."[16]

This book demonstrates that since her role as Nurturer and Preserver of the Family has been central to the idea of woman in our culture, her "criminality" appears directly proportionate to her lack of maternal compassion and self-sacrifice. In the extreme figure of Medea, Fo and Rame expose and critique the assumption that a woman's raison d'être is to be a creature who lives for others, most often encased in the role of wife and mother. They recognize that our horror at Medea's crime is directly related to the fact that she is a mother; why should we demonize Medea for killing her sons, but not Agamemnon for sacrificing his daughter? It is the "naturalness" of feminine self-sacrifice that Rame and Fo assault in *Female Parts*; this play challenges our most basic belief about what it means to be a woman.

"Medea" is the concluding monologue of an evening of tragicomic monologues, performed by Rame, in which she embodies numerous Italian women, including her own self. As Rame steps from one body to another her performance exposes gender as what Elin Diamond calls a "sexual costume, a sign of a role, not evidence of an identity."[17] In the course of one harrowing evening many women emerge through Rame's body—alienated mothers, whores in mental institutions, political prisoners, seductresses, and survivors of rape. All of these women are caught within the suffocating control of patriarchal institutions—the church, the state, marriage, the medical profession—and each tries in her own way to rebel. Their collective anger builds over the course of the evening until the last woman takes the stage; this is Medea, the quintessential rebel, the embodiment of female rage. As the culmination of Rame and Fo's theatrical denaturalization of accepted femininity, this Medea reveals the complex role her vengeful predecessor

(Euripides' Medea) has played in the construction of oppressive gender ideologies. Rame sets up the Medea story in a prologue, describing how this Medea diverges from Euripides' constructed she-monster:

> Tonight's Medea, as played in the hills of Umbria and Tuscany, is a popular Medea which follows the tragic writing of Euripides, but the statement of the reasons for killing the sons is different. This is not a drama of jealousy and wrath as in Euripides. It's a matter of conscience . . . Franca Rame and Dario Fo didn't write this Medea. They discovered it, written in an archaic language, a dialect of central Italy.[18]

In Fo and Rame's "discovered" *Medea*, Euripides' work is set aside as a fiction that misrepresents the lives of real women. Medea as we have come to know her is a construction, a masculine nightmare/fantasy, while Rame and Fo's Medea, they tell us (in the written prologue), is not written at all. Rame distances herself from the role of writer, and by claiming to have *encountered* this Medea, she claims an authenticity for her dramatic interpretation that has eluded those who rely only on written legend. Fo and Rame claim to have found the true explanation for the murder of Medea's children in the real lives of Italian women, and they tell us we will learn to see Medea's "insane crime" as a carefully reasoned response to an insane situation. They will show us that Medea is not an icon for female deviance but is a particular woman, in a particular circumstance, coming to a particularly tragic conclusion about the nature of her life within a patriarchal culture. They claim for their Medea the masculine prerogative of individuality, an individuality grounded in her gendered experience in the material world. Like the complexity of the real Francine Hughes juxtaposed against Farrah Fawcett's simplistic portrayal of her, this Medea promises to be far more difficult to isolate, contain, and control than Euripides' she-monster.

Rame plays all of the parts in this Medea; she is the everywoman of the chorus and she is the callous husband. Rame is a medium for all of the voices, all of the roles. She is the deserted wife, the anxious nurse, and the helpless children. Her body contains the cultural voice of a community, and because Medea emerges at the end of *Female Parts*, all of the other women Rame has played—the rape survivor, the battered wife, the whore—are also present. Medea is infused with women's history of anger, frustration, humor, sorrow, and defiance. When Medea is called upon to temper her anger and think of the children first, she refuses to accept what seems natural to everyone else. "For the love you have for these children, Medea, you must sacrifice. Not as a vain woman but as a worthy mother you ought to think . . . for the good of your own flesh and blood be satisfied" (56). To the everywoman in the chorus the children are Medea's flesh and blood. They do not realize that for Medea her "flesh and blood" is contained first and foremost in her *own* body; like the men in her world she claims the right to protect her own body and soul at all costs. This is the truly subversive message of the play.

Medea sees her sons' murder as her only chance to preserve her own identity in a world that will tolerate her only if she sacrifices herself for others. She understands the implications of her action and knows that forevermore, her name will evoke images of a monstrous woman; still, she will accept the role of martyr if it will empower future women. Medea tries to explain her logic: "Kill I must my sons, thus I will be remembered by all as an unnatural mother and jealous madwoman. But better to be remembered as a ferocious beast than forgotten like a docile goat that one can milk and then despise and sell at market without so much from its mouth as a bleat. I must kill my sons!" (58)

The chorus replies with horror: "Those are not the words of a mother but of a diseased whore, a mad dog!" (58) Medea replies: "Outside people will shout 'Monster, and bitch and evil unnatural mother.' And I will say to myself, weeping (*half voice*) Die, die to give birth to a woman! (*high voice*) Die! To give birth to a woman" (60). Fo and Rame's Medea is a martyr willing to be despised but insisting upon being acknowledged. She accepts the role of monster in order to "give birth to a new woman," a woman freed from the assumption that without sacrificing her own life to the needs and desires of the patriarchy she has no right to exist.

So must we kill our children to free ourselves from oppressive gender roles? Of course not. Rame assures us in her prologue that she is speaking to us on a different level. "Women audience members, it is not suggested that after you see this piece you go home and cut the throats of your children. No this is allegory" (54–55). A stronger woman will raise a stronger child. David Hirst writes that Fo and Rame "demand a full understanding of the circumstances which condition the character's conduct: circumstances which can—and must—be changed."[19] Ultimately Fo and Rame's *Medea* calls for the audience to examine its own participation in the oppression of women and challenges them to change the future. They ask us to view our world critically in light of their political theater, and so I end this book with a return to our most recent Medea figure, Susan Smith.

If we have really listened to Rame's Medea, perhaps we would see this tragic crime in a more political light. Rame's Medea might lead us to ask why Susan Smith's crime was reported on the front page of every U.S. newspaper while, on the same day, a story about a man who decapitated his two sons on a Brooklyn highway warranted only a one-paragraph story on an inside page of the *New York Times*. Rame's Medea might push us to ask why Smith's trial became the focus of national attention while we never read another word about the father who beheaded his children. Rame's Medea would demand to know why television news coverage showed crowds outside of Smith's trial, chanting, "Burn her! Burn her!" while across the continent news programs filmed protesters outside the O. J. Simpson murder trial demanding that the judge and jury "free the Juice." Perhaps Rame's Medea might even prompt us to ask if we, as a culture, bear some responsibility for the death of Smith's two sons. After all, have we not participated in the society that produced Susan Smith, a woman so terrified of being without a man that she killed her children to escape being "alone"?

Dramatic representations of criminal women play an important role in justifying patriarchal oppression of women. The messages women receive through these narratives of containment are entirely gendered. Through these stories women learn that sexual independence is worse than murder (Alice Arden and Ruth Snyder), that self-sacrifice is all that stands between us and death (Mary Edmondson and Francine Hughes), and that pursuing our own desires instead of subsuming them to our children is atrocious (Deborah Eappen). When women assert their right to sexual self-determination, self-governance, sexual and economic independence, they are criminalized; men are not. These gendered instructions are not merely limiting, they can be extremely dangerous. It is no coincidence that there is a recurring theme of domestic violence in these women's crimes and their representations; followed to its painful extreme, the principle of feminine self-sacrifice can result in women enduring emotional and physical abuse in order to maintain family unity.

Medea's daughters are women who did not put others first, whether husbands, parents, or children. They violated the primal patriarchal condition of femininity: self-sacrifice. Fo and Rame's radical Medea is an attempt to pave the way for a new woman in the next millennium: a woman both vulnerable and decisive, self-interested and self-sacrificing. Entitled to her rage, possessed of an anger that may be acknowledged as a necessary assertion of self. Ever hopeful, I envision a future where women's experiences are granted the same cultural validity as men's. And so I wonder, if this does indeed happen in a postmodern, postfeminist age, will we still need Medea to certify the veracity of "unnatural" womanhood, thereby reinforcing the naturalness of a constructed female docility?

In this new millennium I hope that we will have found the ways to address and redress female anger. Then Medea can exit the stage and leave us in peace. Until we honor the rage that is born of oppression, Medea will haunt us and harangue us, and each night the children will die again.

afterword

andrea yates:
a reluctant medea

A WEEK AFTER this book was completed, a young Texas housewife was convicted of first-degree murder after confessing to drowning her five children. Though to my knowledge, as of this writing there has been no dramatic representation of the case in play, movie, or television form, the trial itself could certainly be read as a dramatic narrative. *Court TV* followed the case in detail as did every major newspaper and every network news program. In the twenty-first century we are still fascinated and horrified by the specter of Medea.

It is not my intent here to analyze this case, but I do want to point to the possibility of a change in the traditional rhetoric surrounding women who kill. Though several columnists called for her execution as a "despicable murderer,"[1] most people believed Andrea Yates to be mentally ill and in need of treatment rather than death. She was a woman who had twice attempted suicide and who had been hospitalized four times, most recently with a diagnosis of postpartum psychosis. Though a discourse of gender certainly resonates throughout the case, it was never the defining theme of the debate. Though the Texas branch of the National Organization for Women (NOW) came out in support of Yates as a woman who needed treatment for her mental illness, the discussion of gender was far outweighed in this case by the debate about the insanity plea and standards of responsibility under Texas law. The rhetoric of right-wing columnists who attacked NOW because of its support of Yates or who tried to frame the issue as one of unfair double standards that punish men more severely than women for equal violence,[2] seemed to remain in the periphery of the cultural dialogue.

One aspect of the case does deserve attention in light of this book's analysis. One of the key prosecution witnesses was psychiatrist Park Dietz, who testified that Andrea understood the difference between right and wrong when she drowned her children. He also testified that Andrea told him she had gotten the idea of how to kill the children from an episode of *Law & Order*, a show for which Dietz was a frequent advisor.[3] Later, defense attorneys discovered that the episode Dietz had referred to actually aired after the death of the children, and when confronted with this information Dietz admitted that Yates had never actually said anything to him about the show.[4] It will be interesting to see if the *Law & Order* episode based upon the Yates case (and surely there will be one) references its own participation in her conviction.

There is no doubt that a television movie will emerge; Andrea Yates has already sold the book and movie rights to her story in order to raise money for her defense. What I wonder is what that movie will tell us about the woman who drowned her children because Satan told her that "they were not righteous."[5] Will she be portrayed as villain or victim? Or will we have learned by then that clinging to those simplistic binaries may help us feel safer in the world, but it will not help us save the children.

notes

notes to introduction

1. Phyllis Chesler, *Mothers on Trial: The Battle of Children and Custody* (New York: McGraw Hill, 1986), 44.
2. Elaine Aston, *An Introduction to Feminism and Theatre* (London: Routledge, 1995), 16.
3. Charlotte Canning, "'I Am a Feminist Scholar': The Performative of Feminist History," *Theatre Research International* 26 (2001): 226.
4. Annette Kuhn, "The Power of the Image," in *Media Studies: A Reader*, 2d ed., ed. Paul Marris and Sue Thornham (New York: New York University Press, 2000), 66.
5 Toril Moi, *Sexual/Textual Politics: Feminist Literary Theory* (New York: Metheun, 1985), 44–45.
6. Stuart Hall, "Racist Ideologies and the Media," in *Media Studies: A Reader*, 2d ed., ed. Paul Marris and Sue Thornham (New York: New York University Press, 2000), 272.
7. Canning, "'I Am a Feminist Scholar,'" 226.
8. W. B. Worthen, *The Harcourt Brace Anthology of Drama*, 3d ed. (Berkeley: University of California Press, 2000), 63.
9. As cited in Worthen, *The Harcourt Brace Anthology of Drama*, 64.
10. Lesley Ferris, *Acting Women: Images of Women in Theater* (New York: New York University Press, 1989), 126.
11. Janice Schuetz, *The Logic of Women on Trial: Case Studies of Popular American Trials* (Carbondale: Southern Illinois University Press, 1994), 3.
12. Victor E. Kappeler, Mark Blumberg, and Gary W. Potter, *The Mythology of Crime and Criminal Justice*, 2d ed. (Prospect Heights: Waveland Press, Inc., 1996), 20–21.
13. Ibid., 18–23.
14. Ibid., 20–21.
15. Kathleen Daly, *Gender, Crime and Punishment* (New Haven, Conn.: Yale University Press, 1994), 125.
16. Catherine A. MacKinnon, *Toward a Feminist Theory of the State* (Cambridge, Mass.: Harvard University Press, 1989), 162.
17. Catherine A. MacKinnon, "Feminism, Marxism, Method and the State: Toward a Feminist Jurisprudence," in *Violence Against Women: The Bloody Footprints*, ed. Pauline B. Bart and Eileen Geil Moran (London: Sage Publications, 1993), 213.
18. Judith Lowder Newton, "History as Usual?: Feminism and the 'New Historicism,'" in *The New Historicism*, ed. H. Aram Veeser (London: Routledge, 1989), 152–67.

19. Timothy Roche, "Andrea Yates More to the Story," *Time*, http://www.time.com/time/nation/printout/0,8816,218445,00.html.

20. Kuhn, "The Power of the Image," 67.

notes to chapter 1

1. Francis E. Dolan, "Home-Rebels and House-Traitors: Murderous Wives in Early Modern England," *Yale Journal of Law & the Humanities* 4, no. 1 (winter 1992): 3.

2. The name of the town appears in various accounts as Feversham and Faversham. For consistency I will use the latter spelling.

3. Frances E. Dolan, *Dangerous Familiars: Representations of Domestic Crime in England, 1550–1700* (Ithaca, N.Y.: Cornell University Press, 1994), 21. This book is an invaluable resource to anyone interested in the topic of domestic violence in Renaissance England. I rely heavily on Ms. Dolan's insightful analysis.

4. Frances E. Dolan, "The Subordinate('s) Plot: Petty Treason and the Forms of Domestic Rebellion," *Shakespeare Quarterly* 43, no. 2 (fall 1992): 318.

5. Anita Loomba, *Gender, Race and Renaissance Drama* (Manchester: Manchester University Press, 1989), 67.

6. Catherine Belsey, *The Subject of Tragedy: Identity and Difference in Renaissance Drama* (London: Metheun, 1985), 135.

7. Ibid.

8. Anne Sanders murdered her husband in 1573. Representations of this murder include an extant pamphlet from 1573 and another from 1577; the murder is noted in Holinshed's *Chronicles* and Stow's *A View of Sundry Examples* (1580); finally, there is the anonymous play *Warning for Faire Women* (1590) and a ballad (1592).

9. H. Aram Veeser, *The New Historicism* (New York: Routledge, 1989), xi.

10. Carlo Ginzburg, *Ecstasies: Deciphering the Witches' Sabbath*, trans. Raymond Rosenthal (New York: Pantheon, 1991), 10.

11. Arden's name is spelled Ardern in official accounts.

12. M. L. Wine, introduction to *The Tragedy of Master Arden of Faversham* (London: Metheun, 1973), xxxvii.

13. Ibid.

14. Joseph H. Marshburn, *Murder and Witchcraft in England, 1550–1640: As Recounted in Pamphlets, Ballads, Broadsides and Plays* (Norman: University of Oklahoma Press, 1971), 6.

15. Wine, introduction, 160–62.

16. And the play, in turn, is the source for the extant ballad (1633), Lillo's version of the play (1739), a puppet show (1736), and a ballet at Saddler's Wells (1799).

17. Wine, introduction, 155.

18. *Arden of Faversham* (anonymous) in *Elizabethan Drama*, edited with introductions by John Gassner and William Green (New York: Applause Theatre Book Publishers, 1990), 5. All future references in the text are from this edition; page numbers are noted parenthetically in the text.

19. Edmund Tilney, *The Flower of Friendship: A Renaissance Dialogue Contesting Marriage*, ed. Valerie Wayne (Ithaca, N.Y.: Cornell University Press, 1992), 14.

20. Loomba, *Gender, Race and Renaissance Drama*, 88.

21. Lisa Jardine, *Still Harping on Daughters: Women and Drama in the Age of Shakespeare* (Sussex: The Harvester Press, 1983), 77.

22. Ruth Kelso, *Doctrine for the Lady of the Renaissance* (Chicago: University of Illinois Press, 1978), vii.

23. Dolan, *Dangerous Familiars*, 89.

24. Ibid., 119.
25. Dolan, "Home-Rebels and House-Traitors," 8.
26. Dolan, *Dangerous Familiars*, 99.
27. Dolan, "Home-Rebels and House-Traitors," 13.
28. Ibid., 12–13.
29. Ibid., 15.
30. Tama Starr, *The Natural Inferiority of Women: Outrageous Pronouncements by Misguided Males* (New York: Poseidon Press, 1991), 132–33.
31. *Yorkshire Tragedy*, ed. A. C. Cawley and Barry Gaines (Manchester: Manchester University Press, 1986), 54. All further references to the play are from this edition, and page numbers are indicated parenthetically.
32. Wine, introduction, lxxii.
33. George Lillo, *Arden of Feversham* (1739) anthologized in *The British Drama: Volume First, Tragedies* (London: William Miller, 1804), 520. All further references to the play are from this text, and page numbers are cited parenthetically.

notes to chapter 2

1. Mary S. Hartman, *Victorian Murderess* (New York: Simon and Schuster, 1978), 339.
2. Jerome K. Jerome, *Stageland: Curious Habits and Customs of Its Inhabitants* (New York: Henry Holt and Company, 1890), 37.
3. Jerome, *Stageland*, 71.
4. Ibid., 80–81.
5. Ibid., 71.
6. The numerous crime dramas of the period are well documented in H. Chance Newton, *Crime and the Drama; or Dark Deeds Dramatized* (London: Stanley Paul & Co. Ltd., 1929).
7. According to the census of 1851, as many as 30 percent of women aged twenty to forty were unmarried. Joan Perkin, *Women and Marriage in Nineteenth-Century England* (London: Routledge, 1989), 226.
8. Tama Starr, *The Natural Inferiority of Women: Outrageous Pronouncements by Misguided Males* (New York: Poseidon Press, 1991), 145.
9. Mrs. Henry Wood, *East Lynne* (Boston: George M. Baker & Co., 1865), 27.
10. Hartman, *Victorian Murderess*, 94.
11. Virginia B. Morris, *Double Jeopardy: Women Who Kill in Victorian Fiction* (Lexington: University Press of Kentucky, 1990), 52.
12. Morris, *Double Jeopardy*, 30.
13. Lucia Zedner, *Women, Crime and Custody in Victorian England* (Oxford: Clarendon Press, 1991), 43.
14. Cesare Lombroso, *The Female Offender* (New York: D. Appleton and Co., 1898), 139.
15. Ibid., 86.
16. Ibid., 95.
17. Havelock Ellis, *The Criminal* (London: The Walter Scott Publishing Co. Ltd., 1903), 264.
18. Ibid.
19. Ibid.
20. Frank McLynn, *Crime and Punishment in Eighteenth-Century England* (London: Routledge, 1989), 129.
21. Russel J. Stephens, "William Bodham Donne: Some Aspects of His Later Career as Examiner of Plays," *Theatre Notebook* 35, no. 1 (autumn 1970), 25–32.

22. Tracy C. Davis, *Actresses as Working Women: Their Social Identity in Victorian Culture* (London: Routledge, 1991), 106.

23. *The London Stage 1800–1900: A Documentary Record and Calendar of Performances*, ed. Joseph Donohue (New York: Greenwood Press 1990), 79.

24. Ibid., 83.

25. Lincoln B. Faller, *Turned to Account: The Forms and Functions of Criminal Biography in Late Seventeenth and Early Eighteenth Century England* (Cambridge: Cambridge University Press, 1987), 2.

26. Andrew Knapp and William Baldwin, *The Newgate Calendar: Volume 2* (London: J. Robins and Co., 1825), 245.

27. Ibid., 246.

28. Ibid.

29. Ibid.

30. Ibid.

31. Faller, *Turned to Account*, 37.

32. Ibid.

33. Clarke, who was married to Mary's twin sister, did not defend her innocence but declared that "only God could ever know whether she had done it or not, and if she had, why she had not confessed." Ibid., 36.

34. Ibid., 35.

35. Ibid., 33.

36. C. H. Hazelwood, *Mary Edmonstone* (London: Samuel French, 1862), 3. All quotations from the play are taken from this edition and page numbers are noted parenthetically in the text.

37. Wood, *East Lynne*, 27.

38. The average sentence received by wife beaters was seven to fourteen days, whereas the average sentence for a woman convicted of assault was three months. James A. Hammerton, *Cruelty and Companionship: Conflict in Nineteenth-Century Married Life* (London: Routledge, 1992), 47.

39. Robert Leach, *The Punch and Judy Show: History, Tradition and Meaning* (London: Batsford Academic and Educational, 1985), 41–42.

40. Ellis, *The Criminal*, 299.

41. Cited in Morris, *Double Jeopardy: Women Who Kill in Victorian Fiction*, 42.

42. In the late nineteenth century arsenic was considered to be an aphrodisiac when taken in small doses. It was also used to treat venereal diseases.

43. Maurice Moiseiwitsch, *Five Famous Trials* (Greenwich: New York Graphic Society Publishers, Ltd., 1962), 31.

44. Mary S. Hartman, *Victorian Murderesses* (New York: Simon & Schuster, 1977), 300.

45. Ibid., 321–22.

46. Ibid.

47. Newton, *Crime and the Drama; or Dark Deeds Dramatized*, 29.

48. Hartman, *Victorian Murderesses*, 335.

49. Ibid., 336.

50. Ibid.

notes to chapter 3

1. This title is an homage to Susan Glaspell's short story by the same name, a story that also appeared in the theater as the one-act play *Trifles*. For an excellent analysis of Glaspell's play, which is also based upon a real murder trial, see Linda Ben-Zvi, "Murder

She Wrote: The Genesis of Susan Glaspell's *Trifles*," *Theater Journal* 44 (1992): 141–62.

2. Mary Austin, *The Young Woman Citizen* (New York: The Woman's Press, 1920), 19.

3. Henry Wynans Jessup, *Law for Wives and Daughters: Their Rights and Obligations* (New York: The Macmillan Company, 1927), 4.

4. Ishbel Ross, *Ladies of the Press* (New York: Harper and Brothers Publishers, 1936), 232.

5. *New York Times*, 26 March 1927: 1.

6. Treadwell did not officially cover the case for any newspaper.

7. Ann Jones, *Women Who Kill* (New York: Holt, Rinehart and Winston, 1980), 260.

8. The *New York Herald Tribune* referred to this phenomenon as "psychpathia suburbis."

9. W. L. George, *The Intelligence of Woman* (Boston: Little, Brown and Company, 1920), 87.

10. Alfred Cahen, *Statistical Analysis of American Divorce* (New York: Columbia University Press, 1932), 21.

11. Ibid., 112.

12. Ibid., 60.

13. George, *The Intelligence of Woman*, 13.

14. Ibid.

15. Ibid.

16. Ibid.

17. Ibid., 64.

18. John Kobler, *The Trial of Ruth Snyder and Judd Gray* (New York: Doubleday, Doran & Co. Inc., 1938), 353.

19. *New York Times*, 13 January 1928, p. 2.

20. John Mosedale, *The Men Who Invented Broadway: Damon Runyon, Walter Winchell and Their World* (New York: Richard Marek Publishers, 1981), 155.

21. *New York Times* editorial, 23 April 1927, p. 26.

22. Kobler, *The Trial of Ruth Snyder and Judd Gray*, 39.

23. Ibid., 278.

24. Jones, *Women Who Kill*, 261.

25. Kobler, *The Trial of Ruth Snyder and Judd Gray*, 206.

26. Ibid., 303.

27. Jones, *Women Who Kill*, 257.

28. Ibid., 256.

29. Kobler, *The Trial of Ruth Snyder and Judd Gray*, 342.

30. George, *The Intelligence of Woman*, 13.

31. *New York Times*, 10 May 1927, p. 21.

32. Barbara Belford, *Brilliant Bylines: A Biographical Anthology of Notable Newspaperwomen in America* (New York: Columbia University Press, 1986), 245.

33. Ross, *Ladies of the Press*, 198.

34. Loren Baritz, *The Culture of The Twenties* (Indianapolis: The Bobbs-Merrill Co. Inc., 1970), 419.

35. Jones, *Women Who Kill*, 265.

36. Kobler, *The Trial of Ruth Snyder and Judd Gray*, 55.

37. *New York Evening Post*, 3 May 1927, p. 21.

38. Sophie Treadwell, *Machinal*, in *Plays by American Women 1900–1930*, ed. Judith E. Barlow (New York: Applause Theatre Book Publishers, 1985), 173. All further references to the play are from this edition, and page numbers are cited parenthetically in the text.

39. Kobler, *The Trial of Ruth Snyder and Judd Gray*, 1.

40. Ibid., 263.

41. Ibid., 39.

42. Ibid., 316.
43. Brooks Atkinson, "A Tragedy of Submission," *New York Times*, 8 September 1928, p. 10.
44. Robert Littell, "Chiefly About *Machinal*," *Theatre Arts Monthly* 12, no. 2 (November 1928): 776–77.
45. Ibid.
46. Abraham Myerson, *The Nervous Housewife* (Boston: Little, Brown and Company, 1920), 190–91.
47. Ibid., 191.
48. Jones, *Women Who Kill*, 286.

notes to chapter 4

1. By 1977 *The Total Woman* had sold three million copies. "Fighting the Housewife Blues," *Time*, 14 March 1977, p. 63.
2. Ibid.
3. Marabel Morgan, *The Total Woman* (New York: Pocket Books, 1973), 96–97.
4. Ibid., 64.
5. Ibid., 20.
6. Ibid., 60.
7. "Fighting the Housewife Blues," p. 63.
8. "The End of an ERA?" *Newsweek*, 19 June 1978, p. 34.
9. Untitled news item, *New York Times*, 1 November 1977, p. 16.
10. Angela Browne, *When Battered Women Kill* (New York: The Free Press, 1987), 10.
11. Jerrold Footlick and Elaine Sciolino, "Wives Who Batter Back," *Newsweek*, 3 January 1978, p. 54.
12. Faith McNulty, *The Burning Bed: The True Story of an Abused Wife* (New York: Avon Books, 1980), 24.
13. Ibid.
14. Ibid., 70.
15. Ibid., 132.
16. Ibid., 138.
17. Ibid., 92.
18. Ibid., 105.
19. Ibid., 133.
20. Ibid., 267.
21. Elizabeth M. Schneider and Susan B. Jordan, "Representation of Women Who Defend Themselves in Responses to Physical or Sexual Assault," *Women's Rights Law Reporter* 4, no. 3 (spring 1978): 149–64.
22. Footlick and Sciolino, "Wives Who Batter Back."
23. "A Killing Excuse," *Time*, 28 November 1977, p. 108.
24. Lenore Walker, *Terrifying Love: Why Battered Women Kill and How Society Responds* (New York: Harper and Row Publishers, 1989), 33.
25. McNulty, preface to *The Burning Bed* (no page number).
26. "Who's the Farrahest?" *Newsweek*, 27 June 1977, p. 58.
27. Tom Seligson, "She's Changed, Like It or Not," Interview with Farrah Fawcett, *Redbook*, November 1984, p. 136.
28. Yarmey, in his study "Facial Stereotypes of Battered Women and Battered Women Who Kill," found that "Women categorized as most likely to be battered and most likely to kill their abuser were judged less physically attractive and less likable." *Journal of Applied Social Psychology* 25, no. 4: 344.

29. Stephen Farber, "A Change of Pace for Farrah Fawcett," *New York Times*, 14 May 1984, p. C13.
30. Richard Zoglin, "A Domestic Reign of Terror," *Time* magazine, 8 October 1984, p. 85.
31. Jennifer Regan, "Farrah Proves She's a Serious Actress in a Searing Film Drama," *New York Post*, 8 October 1984, p. 70.
32. McNulty, *The Burning Bed*, 228.
33. Jane Hall, "Farrah Talks About Her Role of a Lifetime," *People Weekly* 164, no. 15 (8 October 1984): 109–110.
34. McNulty, *The Burning Bed*, 258.
35. Cynthia K. Gillespie, *Justifiable Homicide: Battered Women, Self-Defense and the Law* (Columbus: The Ohio State University Press, 1989), 11.
36. Pat Lowry, "The Burning Bed," *Homewatch*, 8 October 1984, p. 56.
37. Ibid., 56.
38. Kay Gardella, "Farrah Fawcett Portrays a Beaten Woman," *TV Week*, 8 October 1984, p. 2.
39. Marvin Kitman, "Fawcett as a Beaten Wife in 'Bed' of Pain," *Newsday*, 8 October 1984, p. 28.
40. Ibid.
41. Pamela Jenkins and Barbara Davidson, "Battered Women in the Criminal Justice System: An Analysis of Gender Stereotypes," *Behavioral Sciences and the Law* 8 (1990): 161.
42. Gillespie, *Justifiable Homicide*, xi.
43. Catherine MacKinnon, "Feminism, Marxism, Method and the State: Toward a Feminist Jurisprudence," in *Violence Against Women: The Bloody Footprints*, ed. Pauline B. Bart and Eileen Geil Moran (Newbury Park: Sage Publications, 1993). See also Deborah L. Rhode, *Justice and Gender: Sex Discrimination and the Law* (Cambridge, Mass.: Harvard University Press, 1989).
44. Lorraine Radford, "Pleading for Time: Justice for Battered Women Who Kill," in *Moving Targets: Women, Murder and Representation* (Berkeley: University of California Press, 1994), 195.
45. Anne M. Coughlin, "Excusing Women," *California Law Review* 82, no. 1 (January 1994): 1.
46. Kandel Mandouche, "Women Who Kill Their Batterers Are Getting Battered in Court," *Ms.* 4, no. 1 (July/August 1993): 88.
47. Tom Carson, "Till Death Do Us Part," *The Village Voice*, 9 October 1984, p. 57.
48. Gioia Diliberto, "A Violent Death, a Haunted Life," *People*, 8 October 1984, p. 100.
49. Ibid., 102.
50. Ibid.
51. Ibid.
52. Ibid.
53. Ibid., 105.
54. Ibid., 106.
55. Ibid.
56. *LA Daily News*, 3 July 1994, p. 13.
57. Rhode, *Justice and Gender*, 238.
58. Browne, *When Battered Women Kill*, 11.
59. Sue E. Eisenberg and Patricia Micklow, "The Assaulted Wife: Catch-22 Revisited," *The Women's Rights Law Reporter* 3, no. 4: 168.
60. Martin D. Schwartz and Walter S. DeKeseredy, "The Return of the Battered Husband Syndrome Through the Typification of Women as Violent," *Crime, Law and Social Change* 20 (1993): 260.

61. Julie Blackman, "Emerging Images of Severely Battered Women and the Criminal Justice System," *Behavioral Sciences and the Law* 8 (1990): 121.

62. Daniel A. Yarmey, "Facial Stereotypes of Battered Women and Battered Women Who Kill," *Journal of Applied Social Psychology* 25, no. 4 (15 February 1995): 348.

notes to chapter 5

1. Katha Pollitt, interview with Deborah Eappen, "Killer Moms, Working Nannies," *The Nation*, 24 November 1997. http://www.thenation.com/issue/971124/1124poll.htm.

2. Charles Patrick Ewing, *Fatal Families: The Dynamics of Intrafamilial Homicide* (London: Sage Publications 1997), 7–8.

3. Annalee Newitz, "Murdering Mothers," in *Bad Mothers: The Politics of Blame in Twentieth-Century America*, ed. Molly Ladd-Taylor and Laurie Umansky (New York: New York University Press, 1998), 336.

4. Ronald L. Goldfarb, *TV or Not TV: Television, Justice and the Courts* (New York: New York University Press, 1998), 144.

5. Paul Thaler, *The Watchful Eye: American Justice in the Age of the Television Trial* (Westport, Conn.: Praeger Publishers, 1994), 13.

6. Danielle Crittenden, *What Our Mothers Didn't Tell Us: Why Happiness Eludes the Modern Woman* (New York: Simon & Schuster, 1999), 129, 134.

7. Anne Scadding, "Au pair pleads not guilty; infant's injuries detailed," *Newton Graphic*, 13 March 1997. http://www.townonline.com/newton/oldarchive/031397/029686 _0_au_031397_5c6cd43f2d.html.

8. Ann-Janine Morey, *What Happened to Christopher: An Anerican Family's Story of Shaken Baby Syndrome* (Carbondale: Southern Illinois University Press, 1998), 10.

9. Deborah Eappen and Terry McCarthy, "One Mother's Story," *The Nation*, 24 November 1997. http://cgi.pathfinder.com/time/magazine/1997/dom/971124/nation.one _mothers_s.html.

10. Pollitt, "Killer Moms, Working Nannies."

11. Ibid.

12. "'Hot Flash' Mothers Who Think," *Salon*. http://www.salonmagazine.com/mwt/hot /1997/10/31hot.html.

13. "American Dream on Trial." http://www.enterspace.org/louise/opinions/1.htm.

14. Dawn Keetley, "Law and Order," in *Prime Time Law: Fictional Television as Legal Narrative*, ed. Robert M. Jarvis and Paul R. Joseph (Durham, N.C.: Carolina Academic Press, 1998), 45.

notes to chapter 6

1. Cynthia K. Gillespie, *Justifiable Homicide: Battered Women, Self-Defense and the Law* (Columbus: Ohio State University Press, 1989), 114.

2. Judith Butler, *Gender Trouble* (London: Routledge, 1990), 270.

3. Ibid., 271.

4. Sophie Treadwell, *Machinal*, 173.

5. Ann Jones, *Women Who Kill* (New York: Holt, Rinehart and Winston, 1980), 226.

6. Ibid., 233.

7. Ibid., 231.

8. Ibid., 222.

9. Ibid., 215.

10. Ibid.

11. Agnes de Mille, *Lizzie Borden: A Dance of Death* (Boston: Little, Brown and Company, 1968), 74.

12. Jones, *Women Who Kill*, 223.

13. All citations from the play come from Sharon Pollock, *Blood Relations and Other Plays* (Edmonton: NeWest Press, 1981). Page numbers cited parenthetically refer to this text.

14. Ibid., 7.

15. *Female Parts* has been adapted by Estelle Parsons and was performed in New York as *Adulto Orgasmo Escapes from the Zoo*.

16. David Hirst, *Dario Fo and Franca Rame* (New York: St. Martin's Press, 1989), 112.

17. Elin Diamond, "Brechtian Theory/Feminist Theory: Toward a Gestic Feminist Criticism," in *A Sourcebook of Feminist Theatre and Performance*, ed. Carol Martin (London, Routledge, 1996), 123.

18. Franca Rame and Dario Fo, *Adulto Orgasmo Escapes from the Zoo*, adapted by Estelle Parsons (New York: Broadway Play Publishing, 1985), 57.

19. Hirst, *Dario Fo and Franca Rame*, 111.

notes to afterword

1. Janelle Brown, "Swift Injustice," *Salon*. http://archive.salon.com/mwt/feature/2002/03/13/yates_reacts/print.html.

2. Dave Kopel, "Bigotry of Low Expectations," *National Review Online*. http://www.nationalreview.com/kopel/kopelprint082801.html.

3. Timothy Roche, "Andrea Yates: More to the Story," *Time*, http://www.time.com/time/nation/printout/0,8816,218445,00.html.

4. Ibid.

5. Ellen Goodman, "Mad Mothers and Angry Fathers," *Washington Post* Writer's Group. http://www.postwritersgroup.com/archives/good0226.htm.

bibliography

Abramson, Phyllis Leslie. *Sob Sister Journalism*. New York: Greenwood Press, 1990.
Altick, Richard D. *Victorian Studies in Scarlet*. New York: W. W. Norton & Co. Inc., 1970.
"American Dream on Trial." http://www.enterspace.org/louise/opinions/1.html.
Aston, Elaine. *An Introduction to Feminism and Theatre*. London: Routledge, 1995.
Atkinson, Brooks."Against the City Clatter." *New York Times*, 16 September 1928, p. 11.
———. "A Tragedy of Submission." *New York Times*, 8 September 1928, p. 10.
Atwell, David. "Property, Status, and the Subject in a Middle-Class Tragedy: *Arden of Feversham*." *English Literary Renaissance* 21, no. 3 (autumn 1991): 328–48.
Austin, Mary. *The Young Woman Citizen*. New York: The Woman's Press, 1920.
Barak, Gregg. "Media, Crime and Justice: A Case for Constitutive Criminology." In *Cultural Criminology*. Boston: Northeastern University Press, 1995.
Baritz, Loren. *The Culture of The Twenties*. Indianapolis: The Bobbs-Merrill Co. Inc., 1970.
Barlow, Judith E. *Plays by American Women 1900–1930*. New York: Theatre Books Publishers, 1985.
Bart, Pauline B., and Eileen Geil Moran. *Violence Against Women: The Bloody Footprints*. Newbury Park: Sage Publications, 1993.
Belford, Barbara. *Brilliant Bylines: A Biographical Anthology of Notable Newspaperwomen in America*. New York: Columbia University Press, 1986.
Bellamy, John. *Crime and Public Order in England in the Later Middle Ages*. London: Routledge, 1973.
Belsey, Catherine. "Alice Arden's Crime." *Renaissance Drama: New Series 8*, edited by Leonard Barkan. Evanston, Ill.: Northwestern University Press, 1982. 83–102.
———. *The Subject of Tragedy: Identity and Difference in Renaissance Drama*. London: Metheun, 1985.
Ben-Zvi, Linda. "Murder She Wrote: The Genesis of Susan Glaspell's *Trifles*." *Theater Journal* 44 (1992): 141–62.
Berger, Arthur Asa. *Narratives in Popular Culture, Media and Everyday Life*. Thousand Oaks, Calif.: Sage Publications, 1997.
Birch, Helen. *Moving Targets: Women, Murder and Representation*. Berkeley: University of California Press, 1994.
Blackman, Julie. "Emerging Images of Severely Battered Women and the Criminal Justice System." *Behavioral Sciences and the Law* 8 (1990): 121–30.
Brown, Janelle. "Swift Injustice." *Salon*. http://archive.salon.com/mwt/feature/2002/03/13/yates_reacts/print.html.

bibliography

Browne, Angela. *When Battered Women Kill.* New York: The Free Press, 1987.
Browne, Angela, and Kirk R. Williams. "Gender, Intimacy, and Lethal Violence: Trends from 1976 through 1987." *Gender & Society* 7, no. 1 (March 1993): 78–98.
Buckley, Tom. "Critics Assail Linking Feminism with Women in Crime." *New York Times*, 14 March 1976, p. 48.
"Burning Bed Defense Rejected." *Pennsylvania Law Journal Reporter* 10, no. 21 (25 May 1987): 1.
Butler, Judith. *Gender Trouble.* London: Routledge, 1990.
Cahen, Alfred. *Statistical Analysis of American Divorce.* New York: Columbia University Press, 1932.
Canning, Charlotte. "'I Am a Feminist Scholar': The Performative of Feminist History." *Theatre Research International* 26 (2001): 223–32.
Cantwell, Mary. "Lizzie Borden Took an Ax." *New York Times Magazine*, 26 July 1992, pp. 18, 42–44.
Carb, David. "Seen on the Stage." *Vogue*, 27 October 1928, p. 74.
Carson, Tom. "Till Death Do Us Part." *Village Voice*, 9 October 1994, p. 56.
Case, Sue-Ellen. *Feminism and Theatre.* New York: Routledge, 1988.
Chapman, A. Beatrice Wallis, and Mary Wallis Chapman. *The Status of Women Under the English Law.* London: George Routledge & Sons Ltd., 1909.
Chesler, Phyllis. *Mothers on Trial: The Battle of Children and Custody.* New York: McGraw Hill, 1986.
Clark, Anna. "Humanity or Justice? Wifebeating and the Law in the Eighteenth and Nineteenth Centuries." *Regulating Womanhood: Historical Essays on Marriage, Motherhood and Sexuality*, 187–206. London: Routledge, 1992. 187–206.
Clarke, Ida Clyde. *Uncle Sam Needs a Wife.* Philadelphia: The John C. Winston Company, 1925.
Cockburn, J. S. *Crime in England 1550–1800.* Princeton, N.J.: Princeton University Press, 1977.
Cole, Virginia Lee. "The Newspaper and Crime." *The University of Missouri Bulletin* 28, no. 4 (21 January 1927): 1–80.
Coughlin, Anne M. "Excusing Women." *California Law Review* 82, no. 1 (January 1994): 1–93.
Crittenden, Danielle. *What Our Mothers Didn't Tell Us: Why Happiness Eludes the Modern Woman.* New York: Simon & Schuster, 1999.
Cromwell, Otelia. "Thomas Heywood: A Study in the Elizabethan Drama of Everyday Life." *Yale Studies in English*, No. 78. New Haven, Conn.: Yale University Press, 1928.
Daly, Kathleen. *Gender, Crime and Punishment.* New Haven, Conn.: Yale University Press, 1994.
Davis, Tracy C. *Actresses as Working Women: Their Social Identity in Victorian Culture.* London: Routledge, 1991.
———. "Questions for a Feminist Methodology in Theatre History." In *Interpreting the Historical Past: Essays in the Historiography of Performance*, edited by Thomas Postlewait and Bruce A. McConachie. Iowa City: University of Iowa Press, 1989.
de Lauretis, Teresa. *Technologies of Gender: Essays on Theory, Film, and Fiction.* Bloomington: Indiana University Press, 1987.
Diamond, Elin. "Brechtian Theory/Feminist Theory: Toward a Gestic Feminist Criticism." In *A Sourcebook of Feminist Theatre and Performance*, edited by Carol Martin. London: Routledge, 1996.
Diliberto, Gioia. "A Violent Death, a Haunted Life." *People Weekly*, 8 October 1984, pp. 100–106.
Disher, M. Willson. *Blood and Thunder: Mid-Victorian Melodrama and Its Origins.* New York: Haskell House Publishers Ltd., 1974.

―――. *Fairs, Circuses and Music Halls*. London: William Collins, 1942.
―――. *Melodrama: Plots That Thrilled*. New York: The Macmillan Company, 1954.
Doggett, Maeve E. *Marriage, Wife-Beating and the Law in Victorian England*. London: Weidenfeld and Nicolson, 1992.
Dolan, Frances E. *Dangerous Familiars: Representations of Domestic Crime in England, 1550–1700*. Ithaca, N.Y.: Cornell University Press, 1994.
―――. "Gender, Moral Agency, and Dramatic Form in *A Warning For Fair Women*." *Studies in English Literature 1500–1900* 29, no. 2 (spring 1989): 201–218.
―――. "Home-Rebels and House-Traitors: Murderous Wives in Early Modern England." *Yale Journal of Law & the Humanities* 4, no. 1 (winter 1992): 1–32.
―――. "The Subordinate('s) Plot: Petty Treason and the Forms of Domestic Rebellion." *Shakespeare Quarterly* 43, no. 3 (fall 1992): 317–40.
Donohue, Joseph, ed. *The London Stage 1800–1900: A Documentary Record and Calendar of Performances*. New York: Greenwood Press, 1990.
Downs, Donald Alexander. *More Than Victims: Battered Women, the Syndrome Society and the Law*. Chicago: University of Chicago Press, 1996.
Dworkin, Andrea. "Living in Terror: Being a Battered Wife." In *Violence Against Women: The Bloody Footprints*, edited by Pauline B. Bart and Eileen Geil Moran. Newbury Park: Sage Publications, 1993.
Eappen, Deborah, and Terry McCarthy. "One Mother's Story." *The Nation*, 24 November 1997. http://cgi.pathfinder.com/time/magazine/1997/dom/971124/nation.one_mothers_s.html.
Edwards, Susan S. M. *Women on Trial: A Study of the Female Suspect, Defendant and Offender in the Criminal Law and Criminal Justice System*. Manchester: Manchester University Press, 1984.
Eisenberg, Sue E., and Patricia L. Micklow. "The Assaulted Wife: Catch-22 Revisited." *The Women's Rights Law Reporter* 3, no. 4 (spring/summer 1977): 138–61.
Ellis, Havelock. *The Criminal*. London: The Walter Scott Publishing Co. Ltd., 1903.
"The End of an ERA?" *Newsweek*, 19 June 1978, p. 34.
Epstein, Su C. "The New Mythic Monster." In *Cultural Criminology*, edited by Jeff Ferrell and Clinton R. Sanders. Boston: Northeastern University Press, 1995.
Ewing, Charles Patrick. *Fatal Famalies: The Dynamics of Intrafamilial Homicide*. London: Sage Publications, 1997.
Faller, Lincoln B. *Turned to Account: The Forms and Functions of Criminal Biography in Late Seventeenth and Early Eighteenth Century England*. Cambridge: Cambridge University Press, 1987.
Farber, Stephen. "A Change of Pace for Farrah Fawcett." *New York Times*, 14 May 1984, p. C13.
Ferrell, Jeff, and Clinton R. Sanders. *Cultural Criminology*. Boston: Northeastern University Press, 1995.
Ferris, Lesley. *Acting Women: Images of Women in Theater*. New York: New York University Press, 1989.
"Fighting the Housewife Blues." *Time*, 14 March 1977, p. 62–69.
Fiske, John. *Media Matters: Race and Gender in U.S. Politics*. Minneapolis: University of Minnesota Press, 1996.
Footlick, Jerrold, and Elaine Sciolino. "Wives Who Batter Back." *Newsweek*, 3 January 1978, p. 54.
Friedman, Lawrence M. *Crime and Punishment in American History*. New York: Basic Books, 1993.
Gardella, Kay. "Farrah Fawcett Portrays a Beaten Woman." *TV Week*, 8 October 1984, p. 2.

Gassner, John, and William Green. *Elizabethan Drama: Eight Plays*. New York: Applause Theatre Book Publishers, 1990.
George, W. L. *The Intelligence of Woman*. Boston: Little, Brown and Company, 1920.
Gillespie, Cynthia K. *Justifiable Homicide: Battered Women, Self-Defense and the Law*. Columbus: The Ohio State University Press, 1989.
Goldfarb, Ronald L. *TV or Not TV: Television, Justice and the Courts*. New York: New York University Press, 1998.
Goodman, Ellen. "Mad Mothers and Angry Fathers." *Washington Post* Writer's Group. http://www.postwritersgroup.com/archives/good0226.htm.
Grundy, Sydney. *A Fool's Paradise*. London: Samuel French, 1898.
Hadas, Pamela White. *Designing Women*. New York: Alfred A. Knopf, 1979.
Hall, Jane. "Farrah Talks About Her Role of a Lifetime." *People Weekly*, 8 October 1984, pp. 109–10.
Hall, Stuart. "Racist Ideologies and the Media." In *Media Studies: A Reader*, 2d ed., edited by Paul Marris and Sue Thornham, 271–82. New York: New York University Press, 2000.
Halverson, Bruce Rogness. "Arthur Hopkins: A Theatrical Biography." Ph.D. diss., University of Washington, 1971.
Hammerton, James A. *Cruelty and Companionship: Conflict in Nineteenth-Century Married Life*. London: Routledge, 1992.
Hammond, Percy. "The Theatres." *New York Herald Tribune*, 16 September 1928, sec. 8, p. 1.
Hart, Lynda. *Fatal Women: Lesbian Sexuality and the Mark of Aggression*. Princeton, N.J.: Princeton University Press, 1944.
———. "The Victorian Villainess and the Patriarchal Unconscious." *Literature and Psychology* 40, no. 3 (1994): 1–25.
Hartman, Mary S. *Victorian Murderess*. New York: Simon & Schuster, 1978.
Hazelwood, C. H. *Mary Edmonstone*. London: Samuel French, 1862.
Heinzelman, Susan Sage, and Zipporah Batshaw Wiseman. *Representing Women: Law, Literature and Feminism*. Durham, N.C.: Duke University Press, 1994.
Heywood, Thomas. *An Apology for Actors (1612)*. Edited by Richard H. Perkinson. New York: Scholars' Facsimiles & Reprints, 1941.
Higginbotham, Ann R. "Sin of the Age: Infanticide and Illegitimacy in Victorian London." *Victorian Studies* 32, no. 3 (spring 1989): 319–37.
Higginson, Thomas Wentworth. *Common Sense About Women*. Boston: Lee and Shepard Publishers, 1882.
Hirst, David. *Dario Fo and Franca Rame*. New York: St. Martin's Press, 1989.
Hoffer, Peter C., and N. E. H. Hull. *Murdering Mothers: Infanticide in England and New England 1558–1803*. New York: New York University Press, 1981.
Hoffman, Jan. "Domestic Disturbance: 083 in Newark's South Ward." *Village Voice*, 9 October 1984, p. 56.
Hopkins, Arthur. "Ten of My Favorite Plays." *New York Sun*, 26 March 1934, p. 13.
———. *To A Lonely Boy*. New York: Doubleday, 1937.
"'Hot Flash' Mothers Who Think." *Salon*. http://www.salonmagazine.com/mwt/hot/1997/10/31hot.html.
Hyslop, Gabrielle. "Deviant and Dangerous Behavior: Women in Melodrama." *Journal of Popular Culture* 19, no. 3 (winter 1985).
Jacoby, Susan. "Hers." *New York Times Magazine*, 1 December 1977, p. C2.
Jardine, Lisa. *Still Harping on Daughters: Women and Drama in the Age of Shakespeare*. Sussex: The Harvester Press, 1983.
Jenkins, Alan. *The Twenties*. New York: Universe Books, 1974.

Jenkins, Pamela, and Barbara Davidson. "Battered Women in the Criminal Justice System: An Analysis of Gender Stereotypes." *Behavioral Sciences and the Law* 8 (1990): 161–70.
Jerome, Jerome K. *On the Stage and Off: The Brief Career of a Would-be Actor.* Wolfeboro Falls: Alan Sutton Publishing Inc., 1891.
——. *Stageland: Curious Habits and Customs of its Inhabitants.* New York: Henry Holt and Company, 1890.
Jessup, Henry Wynans. *Law for Wives and Daughters: Their Rights and Obligations.* New York: The Macmillan Company, 1927.
Jones, Ann. "The Burning Bed and Man Slaughter." *Women's Rights Law Reporter* 9, no. 4 (fall 1986): 295–98.
——. *Next Time She'll Be Dead: Battering and How to Stop It.* Boston: Beacon Press, 1994.
——. *Women Who Kill.* New York: Holt, Rinehart and Winston, 1980.
Jones, Robert Edmund. *The Dramatic Imagination.* New York: Theatre Arts Books, 1941.
Kandel, Minouche. "Women Who Kill Their Batterers Are Getting Battered in Court." *Ms.* 4, no. 1 (July 1993): 88–89.
Kappeler, Victor E., Mark Blumberg, and Gary W. Potter. *The Mythology of Crime and Criminal Justice.* 2d ed. Prospect Heights: Waveland Press, Inc., 1999.
Kato, Sadahide. "Alice Arden of Feversham and Her Company of Evil." *Poetry and Drama in the Age of Shakespeare: Essays in Honour of Professor Shonosuke Ishii's Seventieth Birthday.* Edited by Peter Milward and Tetsuo Anzai. Tokyo: The Renaissance Institute, 1987. 184–98.
Keetley, Dawn. "Law and Order." In *Prime Time Law: Fictional Television as Legal Narrative,* edited by Robert M. Jarvis and Paul R. Joseph. Durham, N.C.: Carolina Academic Press, 1998.
Kelly, Joan. *Women, History & Theory: The Essays of Joan Kelly.* Chicago: University of Chicago Press, 1984.
Kelso, Ruth. *Doctrine for the Lady of the Renaissance.* Chicago: University of Illinois Press, 1978.
"A Killing Excuse: Expanding the Laws of Self-Defense." *Time,* 28 November 1977, p. 108.
Kitman, Marvin. "Fawcett as a Beaten Wife in a Bed of Pain." *New York Newsday,* 8 October 1984, p. 28.
Knapp, Andrew, and William Baldwin. *The Newgate Calendar: Volume 2.* London: J. Robins and Co., 1825.
Kobler, John. *The Trial of Ruth Snyder and Judd Gray.* New York: Doubleday, Doran & Co. Inc., 1938.
Kopel, Dave. "Bigotry of Low Expectations." *National Review Online.* http://www.nationalreview.com/kopel/kopelprint082801.html.
Krutch, Joseph Wood. "Behaviorism and Drama." *The Nation* 127, no. 329 (26 September 1929): 302.
Kuhn, Annette. "The Power of the Image." In *Media Studies: A Reader,* 2d ed., edited by Paul Marris and Sue Thornham, 62–67. New York: New York University Press, 2000.
Leach, Robert. *The Punch and Judy Show: History, Tradition and Meaning.* London: Batsford Academic and Educational, 1985.
Lieblein, Leanore. "The Context of Murder in English Domestic Plays, 1590–1610." *Studies in English Literature 1500–1900* 23, no. 2 (spring 1983): 181–96.
Lillo, George. "Arden of Feversham." *The British Drama: Volume First, Tragedies,* 520–39. London: William Miller, 1804.
Lincoln, Victoria. *A Private Disgrace: Lizzie Borden by Daylight.* New York: G. P. Putnam and Sons, 1967.

Littell, Robert. "Chiefly About *Machinal*." *Theatre Arts Monthly* 12, no. 2 (November 1928): 774.
Lombroso, Cesare. *The Female Offender*. New York: D. Appleton and Company, 1898.
Loomba, Anita. *Gender, Race and Renaissance Drama*. Manchester: Manchester University Press, 1989.
Lowry, Pat. "The Burning Bed." *Home Watch*, 8 October 1984, p. 56.
Macdonald, Myra. *Representing Women: Myths of Femininity in the Popular Media*. New York: Oxford University Press, 1995.
MacKinnon, Catherine A. "Feminism, Marxism, Method and the State: Toward a Feminist Jurisprudence." In *Violence Against Women: The Bloody Footprints*, edited by Pauline B. Bart and Eileen Geil Moran. London: Sage Publications, 1993.
———. *Toward a Feminist Theory of the State*. Cambridge, Mass.: Harvard University Press, 1989.
Malcolmson, R. W. "Infanticide in the Eighteenth Century." In *Crime in England 1550–1800*, edited by J. S. Cockburn, 187–209. Princeton, N.J.: Princeton University Press, 1977.
"Man Who Burned His Wife is Charged With Murder." *New York Times*, 17 October 1984, p. A16.
Mandouche, Kandel. "Women Who Kill Their Batterers Are Getting Battered in Court." *Ms.* 4, no. 1 (July/August 1993): 88.
Marshburn, Joseph H. *Murder and Witchcraft in England, 1550–1640: As Recounted in Pamphlets, Ballads, Broadsides and Plays*. Norman: University of Oklahoma Press, 1971.
Marshburn, Joseph H., and Alan R. Velie. *Blood and Knavery: A Collection of English Renaissance Pamphlets and Ballads of Crime and Sin*. Rutherford, N.J.: Fairleigh Dickinson University Press, 1973.
McLuskie, Kathleen. *Renaissance Dramatists*. New Jersey: Humanities Press International, Inc., 1989.
McLynn, Frank. *Crime and Punishment in Eighteenth-Century England*. London: Routledge, 1989.
McNulty, Faith. *The Burning Bed: The True Story of an Abused Wife*. New York: Avon Books, 1980.
Messerschmidt, James W. *Capitalism, Patriarchy and Crime: Toward a Socialist Feminist Criminology*. New Jersey: Rowman & Littlefield, 1986.
Minh-ha, Trinh T. *When the Moon Waxes Red: Representation, Gender and Cultural Politics*. New York: Routledge, 1991.
Moi, Toril. *Sexual/Textual Politics: Feminist Literary Theory*. New York: Metheun, 1985.
Moiseiwitsch, Maurice. *Five Famous Trials*. Greenwich: New York Graphic Society Publishers Ltd., 1962.
Mordden, Ethan. *That Jazz! An Idiosyncratic Social History of the American Twenties*. New York: G. P. Putnam's Sons, 1978.
Morey, Ann-Janine. *What Happened to Christopher?: An American Family's Story of Shaken Baby Syndrome*. Carbondale: Southern Illinois University Press, 1998.
Morgan, Arthur Eustace. *English Domestic Drama*. Folcroft: Folcroft Press, Inc., 1912.
Morgan, Marabel. *The Total Woman*. New York: Pocket Books, 1973.
Morley, David. "Cultural Transformations: The Politics of Resistance." In *Media Studies: A Reader*, 2d ed., edited by Paul Marris and Sue Thornham, 471–81. New York: New York University Press, 2000.
Morris, Virginia B. *Double Jeopardy: Women Who Kill in Victorian Fiction*. Lexington: University Press of Kentucky, 1990.
Mosedale, John. *The Men Who Invented Broadway: Damon Runyon, Walter Winchell and Their World*. New York: Richard Marek Publishers, 1981.

Myerson, Abraham. *The Nervous Housewife*. Boston: Little, Brown and Company, 1920.
Nathan, George Jean. "A Pretentious Zero." *The American Mercury* 15 (November 1928): 376.
"New Manner, Old Matter, True Tragedy." *The Boston Transcript* 29 September 1928, p. 6.
Newitz, Annalee. "Murdering Mothers." In *Bad Mothers: The Politics of Blame in Twentieth-Century America*, edited by Molly Ladd-Taylor and Laurie Umansky. New York: New York University Press, 1998.
Newton, H. Chance. *Crime and the Drama; or Dark Deeds Dramatized*. London: Stanley Paul & Co. Ltd., 1929.
Newton, Judith Lowder. "History as Usual?: Feminism and the 'New Historicism.'" In *The New Historicism*, edited by H. Aram Veeser. New York: Routledge, 1989.
———. *Starting Over: Feminism and the Politics of Cultural Critique*. Ann Arbor: The University of Michigan Press, 1994.
New York Times, 21 March 1927 to 15 January 1928.
New York Times, 1 November 1977, p. 16.
New York World, 21 March 1927 to 15 January 1928.
Okin, Susan Moller. *Justice, Gender and the Family*. New York: Basic Books, 1989.
Parent, Jennifer. "Arthur Hopkins' Production of Sophie Treadwell's *Machinal*." *The Drama Review* 26, no. 1 (spring 1982): 87–100.
Perkin, Joan. *Women and Marriage in Nineteenth-Century England*. London: Routledge, 1989.
Pollitt, Katha. "Killer Moms, Working Nannies." *The Nation*. http://www.thenation.com/issue/971124/1124poll.htm.
Pollock, Sharon. *Blood Relations and Other Plays*. Edmonton: NeWest Press, 1981.
Price, Barbara Raffel, and Natalie J. Sokoloff. *The Criminal Justice System and Women: Offender, Victims and Workers*. 2d ed. New York: McGraw-Hill, Inc. 1995.
Radford, Lorraine. "Pleading for Time: Justice for Battered Women Who Kill." In *Moving Targets: Women, Murder and Representation*. Berkeley: University of California Press, 1994.
Rahill, Frank. *The World of Melodrama*. London: Pennsylvania State University Press, 1967.
Rame, Franca, and Dario Fo. *Adulto Orgasmo Escapes from the Zoo*. Adapted by Estelle Parsons. New York: Broadway Play Publishing, 1985.
Regan, Jennifer. "Farrah Proves She's a Serious Actress in a Searing Film Drama." *New York Post*, 8 October 1984, p. 70.
Reske, Henry J. "License to Kill?" *American Bar Association Journal* 79 (April 1993): 37.
Rhode, Deborah L. *Justice and Gender: Sex Discrimination and the Law*. Cambridge, Mass.: Harvard University Press, 1989.
Roche, Timothy. "Andrea Yates More to the Story." *Time*. http://www.time.com/time/nation/printout/0,8816,218445,00.html.
Rosenstine, Robert A. "The Future of the Past: Film and the Beginnings of Postmodern History." In *The Persistence of History: Cinema, Television and the Modern Event*, edited by Vivian Sobchack. New York: Routledge, 1996.
Ross, Ishbel. *Ladies of the Press*. New York: Harper and Brothers, 1936.
Roth, Martha. "Notes Toward a Feminist Performance Aesthetic." *Women and Performance* 1, no. 1 (spring/summer 1983): 5–14.
Sachs, Hannelore. *The Renaissance Woman*. Trans. by Marianne Herzfeld. New York: McGraw-Hill Book Company, 1971.
Sanders, Clinton R., and Eleanor Lyon. "Repetitive Retribution: Media Images and the Cultural Construction of Criminal Justice." In *Cultural Criminology*. Boston: Northeastern University Press, 1995.

Sargeant, Georgia. "Battered Woman Syndrome Gaining Legal Recognition." *Trial* 27, no. 4 (April 1991): 17–20.
Scadding, Anne. "Au pair pleads not guilty; infant's injuries detailed." *Newton Graphic*. http//www.townonline.com/newton/oldarchive/031397/029686_0_au_031397_5c6cd4 3f2d.html.
Schneider, Elizabeth M., and Susan B. Jordan. "Representation of Women Who Defend Themselves in Response to Physical or Sexual Assault." *Women's Rights Law Reporter* 4, no. 3 (spring 1978): 149–64.
Schofield, Ann. "Lizzie Borden Took an Ax: History, Feminism and American Culture." *American Studies* 34, no. 1 (spring 1993): 91–103.
Schueller, Regina, Vicki L. Smith, and James M. Olsen. "Jurors Decisions in Trials of Battered Women Who Kill: The Role of Prior Beliefs and Expert Testimony." *Journal of Applied Social Psychology* 24, no. 4 (1994): 316–37.
Schuetz, Janice. *The Logic of Women on Trial: Case Studies of Popular American Trials*. Carbondale: Southern Illinois University Press, 1994.
Seligson, Tom. "Farrah Fawcett: She's Changed, Like it or Not." *Redbook* 164, no. 1 (November 1984): 138–40.
Shanley, Mary Lyndon. *Feminism, Marriage and the Law in Victorian England 1850–1895*. London: I. B. Taurus & Co. Ltd., 1989.
Sievers, David W. *Freud on Broadway: A History of Psychoanalysis and the American Drama*. New York: Hermitage House, 1955.
Smart, Carol. *Regulating Womanhood: Historical Essays on Marriage, Motherhood and Sexuality*. London: Routledge, 1992.
Smith, Alison. "Mills of the Gods." *New York World*, 10 September 1928, p. 13.
Sparks, Richard. "Entertaining the Crisis: Television and the Moral Enterprise." In *Crime and the Media: The Post-modern Spectacle*, edited by David Kidd-Hewitt and Richard Osborne. London: Pluto Press, 1995.
Spiering, Frank. *Lizzie*. New York: Random House, 1984.
Starr, Tama. *The Natural Inferiority of Women: Outrageous Pronouncements by Misguided Males*. New York: Poseidon Press, 1991.
Stone-Blackburn, Susan. "Feminism and Metadrama: Role-playing in *Blood Relations*." *Canadian Drama* 15, no. 2 (1989): 169–78.
Strand, Ginger. "Treadwell's Neologism: *Machinal*." *Theatre Journal* 44 (1992): 163–75.
Sullivan, Robert. *Goodbye Lizzie Borden*. Brattleboro: The Stephen Greene Press, 1974.
Thaler, Paul. *The Watchful Eye: American Justice in the Age of the Television Trial*. Westport, Conn.: Praeger Publishers, 1994.
Tierney, Kathleen J. "The Battered Women Movement and the Creation of the Wife Beating Problem." *Social Problems* 29, no. 3 (February 1982): 207–20.
Tilney, Edmund. *The Flower of Friendship: A Renaissance Dialogue Contesting Marriage*, edited by Valerie Wayne. Ithaca, N.Y.: Cornell University Press, 1992.
Townsend, Camilla. "I Am the Woman for Spirit: A Working Woman's Transgression in Victorian London." *Victorian Studies* 36, no. 3 (spring 1993): 293–314
The Tragedy of Master Arden of Faversham. Edited by M. L. Wine. London: Methuen & Co. Ltd., 1973.
———. Edited by Martin White. London: Ernest Benn Limited, 1982.
Treadwell, Sophie. "The Hopkins Manner." *New York World*, 25 November 1928, p. 16.
———. "Machinal." *Twenty-Five Best Plays of the Modern American Theatre*, edited by John Gassner. New York: Crown, 1949.
Turenne, Veronique. "Most Serious Injuries Happen After Separation." *Los Angeles Daily News*, 3 July 1994, p. 13.
Veeser, H. Aram. *The New Historicism*. New York: Routledge, 1989.

Walker, Lenore E. *Terrifying Love: Why Battered Women Kill and How Society Responds.* New York: Harper & Row Publishers, 1989.
Walker, Samuel, Cassia Spohn, and Miriam DeLone. *The Color of Justice: Race, Ethnicity and Crime in America.* Belmont, Calif.: Wadsworth Publishing Company, 1996.
"Who's the Farrahest?" *Newsweek,* 27 June 1977, p. 58.
Wiener, Carol Z. "Sex Roles and Crime in Late Elizabethan Hertfordshire." *Journal of Social History* 8, no. 4 (summer 1975): 38–60.
Wilson, Edmund. *The American Earthquake: A Documentary of the Twenties and Thirties.* Garden City, N.Y.: Doubleday Anchor Books, 1958.
Wine, M. L. *The Tragedy of Master Arden of Faversham.* London: Metheun, 1973.
Wolfe, Virginia. *A Room of One's Own.* New York: Harcourt, Brace & World, Inc., 1929.
"Woman Denied Acquittal in Killing of Ex-Husband." *New York Times,* 1 November 1977, p. 16.
Wood, Mrs. Henry. *East Lynne.* Boston: Geo. M. Baker & Co., 1865.
Worthen, W. B. *The Harcourt Brace Anthology of Drama,* 3d ed. Berkeley: University of California Press, 2000.
Yarmey, Daniel A. "Facial Stereotypes of Battered Women and Battered Women Who Kill." *Journal of Applied Social Psychology* 25, no. 4: 338–52.
Yellis, Kenneth A. "Prosperity's Child: Some Thoughts on the Flapper." In *Women's Experience in America: An Historical Anthology,* edited by Esther Katz and Anita Rapone. London: Transaction Books. 1980.
A Yorkshire Tragedy. Edited by A. C. Cawley and Barry Gaines. Manchester: Manchester University Press, 1986.
Young, William C. *Famous Actors and Actresses on the American Stage: Documents of American Theatre History.* New York: R. R. Bowker Company, 1975.
Zedner, Lucia. *Women, Crime, and Custody in Victorian England.* Oxford: Clarendon Press, 1991.
Zichy, Francis. "Justifying the Ways of Lizzie Borden to Men: The Play Within the Play Sharon Pollock's *Blood Relations.*" *Theatre Annual* 1987: 61–81.
Zoglin, Richard. "A Domestic Reign of Terror." *Time,* 8 October 1984, p. 85.

index

Acton, William, 19, 23
adultery, xi, xvi, 1, 6, 8, 11, 16, 17, 18, 36–38, 45, 52, 64, 66, 88
adventuress, 18, 20
"Angel in the House," xvii, 21, 23
Arden, Alice, xiv, xvi–xvii, 1, 3, 4, 6–11, 13, 14–18, 21, 27, 64, 87, 88, 89, 100
Arden, Thomas, 1, 4–11, 15–18
Arden of Faversham, 11, 14, 15, 16, 104
arsenic, 35–36, 106
Aston, Ellen, ix, 103
Atkinson, Brooks, 53, 108
au pair, xviii, 75, 76, 77, 78, 82–84, 86, 110
Aubrey, Mary, 15

Basic Instinct, xiii
Battered Women's Syndrome, 67, 68, 70
Belsey, Catheine, 3, 104
Blackman, Julie, 71, 110
Blood Relations (Pollock), xviii, 89, 90, 95, 96, 111
Bonfire of the Vanities, xiii
Borden, Lizzie, xiv, xviii, 86, 89, 90–96, 111
Borgia, Lucretia, 21
Burning Bed, The (McNulty), xiii, xvii, 58–60, 62–63, 66, 69, 71, 108, 109
Butler, Judith, 89, 110

Cahen, Alfred, 41, 107
Calverley, Walter, 13
Canning, Charlotte, x, xi, 103
Chamberlain, Lord, 26, 27, 33
Charles I, 11, 12

Charlie's Angels, xvii, 63
chastity, 10, 11, 17, 18
Chronicles of England, Scotland, and Wales (Holinshed's), 1, 4–6, 9, 104
Clytemnestra, ix, xii, 15
"Complaint and Lamentation of Mistress Arden of Faversham, The," 4, 6
Court TV, xviii, 75, 77, 78, 80, 81, 101
coverture, 10, 21, 22, 35, 41
Crittenden, Danielle, 77, 110

Darwin, Charles, 25
Davis, Tracy, 26, 106
Diamond, Elin, 97, 111
Dietz, Park, 101–2
Divorce Act, 35
Dolan, Francis, 1, 104, 105

Eappen, Deborah, 76, 77–81, 89, 110
Eappen, Matthew, xviii, 75–76, 78, 83
East Lynne (Wood), 22, 33, 105, 106
Edmondson, Mary, xiv, xvii, 21, 27–30, 32, 33, 47, 88, 100
Edward VI, 1
Ellis, Havelock, 19, 25, 35, 105, 106
Equal Rights Amendment, 57, 108
Euripides, ix, xi, 98

Faller, Lincoln, 27, 106
Fawcett, Farrah, xvii–xviii, 58, 62–63, 65–66, 69, 71, 73, 98, 108, 109
Female Offender (Lombroso), 24
Female Parts, 97, 98, 111
femme couvert, 8, 10, 76
Ferris, Lesley, xii, 103

Fo, Dario, xviii, 97, 98, 100, 111
Fool's Paradise, A, 37, 38

Gassner, John, xi, 104
George, W. L., 40, 107
Gillespie, Cynthia, 65, 67, 109, 110
Gilman, Mildred, 46
Ginzburg, Carlo, 4, 104
Glaspell, Susan, 106, 107
Goodcole, Henry, 12
Gray, (Henry) Judd, 39, 42–44, 46–47, 50–53, 107
Greydanus, Aryan, 58, 71
Grundy, Sydney, 37, 38

Hall, Stuart, xi, 103
Hartman, Mary, 33, 105, 106
Hazelwood, Charles H., 30, 32, 33, 106
Hellish Murder, A, 12
Henry VIII, 5
Hirst, David, 99, 111
History of Crime in England, 23
Hoadley, John, 16
Hopkins, Arthur, 48
Hughes, Francine, xiv, xvii–xviii, 57–71, 73, 88–89, 98, 100
Hughes, Mikey, 58–68, 70

infanticide, 20, 36, 99
Intelligence of Woman, The (George), 40

Jack Sheppard, 19
Jason, xi, 74, 81
Jerome, Jerome K., 20, 105
Johnson, Nunally, 47
Jones, Ann, x, 40, 61, 91, 107, 108, 110, 111
Jones, Robert Edmund, 48
Joyce, Peggy Hopkins, 47–48
Justifiable Homicide (Gillespie), 65, 67, 68, 109, 110

Kappeler, Victor, xiii, 103
Kobler, John, 49, 107
Kuhn, Annette, x, xi, 103, 104

LaFarge, Marie, 21, 27
LaFarge; or, Self-Will in Women, 21, 26
Law & Order, xviii, 75, 76, 81–82, 86, 102
Lillo, George, 16, 17, 18, 104, 105
Littell, Robert, 53, 108

Lombrosian, 25, 45, 57, 74, 87
Lombroso, Cesare, 19, 24, 105
Loomba, Anita, 10, 104

Machinal, xvii, 39, 40, 48–55, 89, 107, 108, 110
Mack, Willard, 45
MacKinnon, Catherine, iv, 103, 109
Married Woman's Property Act, 35
Mary Edmonstone: A Pathetic, Romantic Drama, 30–33, 106
Matrimonial Causes Act, 35
Maybrick, Florence, 36–38
McNulty, Faith, 59–60, 62–63, 65, 108, 109
Medea, ix, xi, xii, xiv, 73, 81, 87, 88, 89, 97–99, 101
Medea (Euripides), xi, 74, 98, 99
Medea (Rame and Fo), xviii, 89, 99, 100
Mill, John Stuart, 34
Moi, Toril, x, 103
Morgan, Marabel, 56–57, 108
Myerson, Abraham, 41, 46, 51, 54, 58, 108

narrative of containment, xii, 11, 81, 90, 96
narrative of resistance, xviii, 88, 89, 90, 94, 97
National Domestic Violence Week, xvii, 58
National Organization for Women (NOW), 101
Nervous Housewife, The (Myerson), 41, 51, 54, 108
New Woman, 40, 41, 42, 46, 54, 100
New York Times, The, 43, 46, 53, 57, 63, 79, 100, 107, 108, 109
Newgate Calendar (Knapp and Baldwin), 27–29, 106
Newits, Annalee, 75, 110
Newton, H. Chance, 37, 105, 106
Newton, Judith, xvi, 103

O'Neil, Nance, 93–94, 96
Owen, M. E., 24

Patmore, Coventry, 21,
patriarchy, ix, xii, xvii, 9, 16, 40, 96, 97, 98, 99, 100
petty treason, xvi, 1, 2, 11, 104

petty tyrant, 12, 15
physiognomy, 24, 25, 35, 45
Picturesque Sketches of London, 35
Pike, Luke Owen, 19, 23
Pollit, Katha, 79, 110
Pollock, Sharon, xviii, 89, 90, 93, 95, 96, 97, 111
postpartum psychosis, 101
Post-traumatic Stress Disorder, 67
Punch and Judy, 34–35

Rame, Frana, xviii, 97, 98, 100, 111
Renaissance, 1, 2, 3, 8, 10–12, 14–16, 104
Ross, Ishbel, 47, 107
Rules of Marriage, 12
Runyon, Damon, 42, 43, 107

Scheck, Barry, 78, 85, 86
Schuetz, Judith, xiii, 103
self-defense, 12, 15, 57, 64, 67, 68, 95
Shaken Baby Syndrome (SBS), 78, 110
Simpson, O. J., 74, 85, 100
Smith, Susan, 73–75, 78–79, 99, 100
Snyder, Albert, 39, 40, 42–46, 48, 50–52
Snyder, Ruth, xiv, xvii–xviii, 39, 40, 42–54, 64, 75, 76, 79, 88–89, 100, 107
Sob Sister, 46
Starr, Tama, 105
Stephens, Justice, 36, 38
Sullivan, Bridget, 91–92, 94
Summary Jurisdiction Act, 35

Tilney, Edmund, 8, 104
Time, 56, 57, 61, 63, 108
Total Woman, The (Morgan), 56–57, 108
Tragedy of Master Arden of Faversham, 4, 6–7, 104
Treadwell, Sophie, xvii, xvii, 39, 40, 48–55, 89, 107, 110
Tyburn, 21, 27

Veeser, H. Aram, 4, 104
Victorian age, xvii, 18–27, 32–36, 38, 105, 106
violence, domestic, xvi, xvii, 3, 11–13, 14, 15, 39, 43–44, 57, 58, 61, 66, 71, 74, 100, 104

Wanrow, Yvonne, 55, 68
Wardmote Book of Faversham, 4–6, 9
Warning for Bad Wives, A, 12
Warning for Faire Women, A, 3, 104
Wine, M. L., 4, 15, 104, 105
Wolstenholme-Elmy, Elizabeth, 36
Woman's Suffrage Reform Bill, 34
Women Who Kill (Jones), x, 40, 61, 107, 108, 110, 111
Woodward, Louise, xiv, xviii, 75–85, 88
Worthen, W. B., xi, 103

Yarmey, Daniel, 71, 108, 110
Yates, Andrea, xviii, 101–2, 104, 111
Yorkshire Tragedy, A, 13, 14, 105

www.ingramcontent.com/pod-product-compliance
Lightning Source LLC
Chambersburg PA
CBHW020748230426
43665CB00009B/538